THE **6** VITAL INGREDIENTS OF SELF-ESTEEM

OF SELF-ESTEEM

How To Develop Them In Your Students

THE 6 VITAL INGREDIENTS OF SELF-ESTEEM

How To Develop Them In Your Students

A Comprehensive Guide for Educators, K-12

By Bettie B. Youngs, Ph.D.

JALMAR PRESS
Rolling Hills Estates, California

THE 6 VITAL INGREDIENTS OF SELF-ESTEEM
How to Develop Them in Your Students:
A Comprehensive Guide for Educators, K-12

Library of Congress Cataloging - in - Publication Data

Youngs, Bettie B.
>The 6 vital ingredients of self-esteem, and how to develop them in your students: a comprehensive guide for educators (K-12) / Bettie B. Youngs.
>
>   p. cm.
>Includes bibliographical references
>ISBN 0-915190-72-9 : $19.95
>1. Students — Psychology. 2. Self-respect in children. 3. Self-respect in adolescence.
>I. Title   II. Title: Six vital ingredients of self-esteem, and how to develop then in your students.
>LB1117.Y64 1992   91-19682
>371.8'1 — dc20   CIP

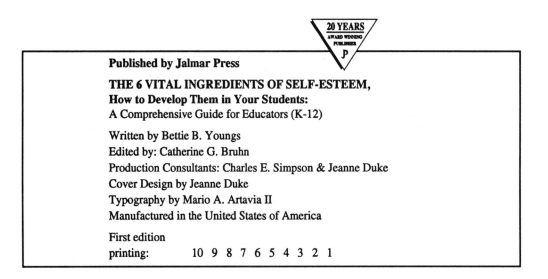

Published by Jalmar Press

THE 6 VITAL INGREDIENTS OF SELF-ESTEEM,
How to Develop Them in Your Students:
A Comprehensive Guide for Educators (K-12)

Written by Bettie B. Youngs
Edited by: Catherine G. Bruhn
Production Consultants: Charles E. Simpson & Jeanne Duke
Cover Design by Jeanne Duke
Typography by Mario A. Artavia II
Manufactured in the United States of America

First edition
printing: 10 9 8 7 6 5 4 3 2 1

THE 6 VITAL INGREDIENTS OF SELF-ESTEEM
How To Develop Them In Your Students

A Comprehensive Guide for Educators, K-12

Self-esteem is a composite of six vital ingredients that can empower or detract from the vitality of our lives. This comprehensive and empowering resource for educators describes these six in detail, and outlines a plan of action for building a child's self-esteem in the schoolplace.

SELF-ESTEEM. The word is used a lot these days, but what is it really? How is it developed in the childhood (K-12) years? What detracts from or empowers it? How is it developed in the schoolplace? How do we educators inspire it in our students? What is the relationship of self-esteem to motivating young people to be productive and achieve successful outcomes, to be happy, to develop healthy and mutual friendships, to truly discover and live out their full potential and to become "fully functional adults?" Self-esteem has been touted to be the cure-all of so much: how can it possibly be so important?

Perhaps you've heard the term *self-esteem* defined as "how much you like your-self." Well, yes, but self-esteem is much, much more than that. Self-esteem is our battery pack. It's a composite of six key ingredients at work in our lives, making up our price tag, so to speak. Self-esteem is the way *we* see ourselves and is very personal. That's why *you* might think a child has everything going for him, but inside, he may not see the same picture. Have you ever looked at a student and thought, "If only Jane knew how capable she is?" "If only Tom knew how bright he is?" How can you help your students develop a healthy self-concept that will yield inner strength and motivation, create a desire to excel and achieve, and unleash potential? Building self-esteem is the key. Nothing affects every aspect of our life, including our health and energy, peace of mind, capabilities, happiness, the quality of our relationships, performance and productivity, the financial goals we set and achieve, our overall success really, quite so much as our self-esteem.

Bettie B. Youngs, Ph.D.

About The Author

Bettie B. Youngs, Ph. D. is an internationally known lecturer, author, counselor and consultant. Her work has spanned more than 60 countries for more than two decades, earning her a reputation as a respected authority in the field of personal and professional effectiveness. She has earned national acclaim for her work on the effects of stress on health, wellness, and productivity for both adults and children. Her work on the role of self-esteem as it detracts from or empowers vitality, achievement and peak performance, as well as her work on the stages of growth and development in the K-12 years and the implications at each stage for the development of self-esteem is exemplary.

Bettie is a former Teacher-of-the-Year, Professor at San Diego State University, Executive Director of the Phoenix Foundation, and currently serves as a consultant to U.S. schools. She is the author of 14 books published in 23 languages, as well as a number of popular audio cassette programs.

Dr. Youngs, a member of the National Speakers Association, addresses audiences throughout the United States and abroad, and meets with nearly 250,000 youth and adults each year. She serves on the Board of Directors for the National Council for Self-Esteem and is a frequent guest on radio and television talk shows. A leader in U.S. education, her consulting firm provides instruction and professional development to school districts nationwide. She may be contacted at:

Bettie B. Youngs & Associates
Instruction & Professional Development, Inc.
3060 Racetrack View Drive
Del Mar, CA 92014
(619) 481-6360

Other Works By Bettie B. Youngs, Ph.D.

BOOKS:

Stress In Children (New York: Avon Books, 1985)

Helping Your Teenager Deal With Stress (New York: Tarcher/St. Martins Press, 1986)

A Stress Management Guide For Young People (San Diego: Learning Tools, 1986)

Is Your Net-Working? A Complete Guide to Building Contacts and Career Visibility
(New York: John Wiley & Sons, 1989)

Friendship Is Forever, Isn't It? (San Diego: Learning Tools, 1990)

Goal Setting Skills for Young Adults (San Diego: Learning Tools, 1990)

Getting Back Together: Creating a New Relationship With Your Partner and Making It Last
(New York: Bob Adams, Inc., 1990)

Problem Solving Skills For Children (San Diego: Learning Tools, 1990)

A Stress Management Guide for Administrators (San Diego: Learning Tools, 1990)

The 6 Vital Ingredients of Self-Esteem: How to Develop Them in Your Child
(New York: Macmillan/Rawson, 1991)

The 6 Vital Ingredients of Self-Esteem: How to Develop Them in Your Students
(Rolling Hills Estates, CA: Jalmar Press, 1992)

Stress Management For Educators (Rolling Hills Estates, CA: Jalmar Press, 1992)

You & Self-Esteem: The Key to Happiness & Success
(Rolling Hills Estates, CA: Jalmar Press, 1992)

Enhancing The Educator's Self-Esteem: Criteria #1
(Rolling Hills Estates, CA: Jalmar Press, 1992)

AUDIO CASSETTES:

Helping Your Teenager Deal With Stress (San Diego: Learning Tools, 1987)

How to Raise Happy, Healthy, Self-Confident Children (Nightengale/Conant, 1990)

The 6 Vital Components of Self-Esteem and How To Develop Them In Your Child
(Sybervision, 1990)

Helping Children Manage Anxiety, Pressure, and Stress (Sybervision, 1991)

Developing Responsibility in Children (Sybervision, 1991)

Getting Back Together (Sybervision, 1991)

To exemplary educators I have been fortunate enough to know: Ardath Bergfall, Glen Pinkham, Ted Kappas, Miss Macklewien, Jon Ericson, Richard Brooks, Dick Sweeney, Chris Christiansen, Gerald Conley, Tom Drake, Diane Peyton, Ruth Glick, Cecil Brewton, J. Bruce Francis, Rita King, Jack Hill, Ron Hockwalt, Mickey Dunaway, Tony Murray, Gerry Rosander

A Note From the Author:

The terms *he* and *she* have been used interchangeably throughout this text. I find the style of using *his* or *her* in the same sentence awkward and encumbering. I hope when you see these terms, and you digest the paragraph where they are used, that visions of your students, whether male or female come to mind. I am talking about *our* students, both boys and girls.

THE 6 VITAL INGREDIENTS OF SELF-ESTEEM
How To Develop Them In Your Students

WHAT OTHERS ARE SAYING ABOUT THIS BOOK:

"Dr. Bettie B. Youngs' newest book is a landmark in the area of developing positive self-esteem in children of all ages. It is critical reading for parents, educators, or anyone who works closely with youth. With this book, Dr. Youngs again teaches us in her insightful, readable, and unmistakably practical style. *The 6 Vital Ingredients of Self-Esteem* crystallizes for the reader the importance of a value-aligned life, and how to build self-esteem from that framework." **Dr. David M. Dunaway, Principal, Benjamin Russell High School, Alexander City, Alabama, 1990 Alabama High School Principal-of-the-Year**

"Dr. Bettie Youngs is exceptionally wise and equally as caring, with a most remarkable gift for teaching us how to become wise and caring, too. This wonderful book combines first-class professional insight with first-class practicality, focusing on the single most important area of concern: healthy self-esteem. I wish all educators and parents would read it." **Dr. Bob Ball, Executive Director, California Task Force to Promote Self-Esteem and Personal and Social Responsibility**

"A healthy self-esteem is one of the greatest gifts we will ever give children. How children feel about themselves determines whether or not they become adults who fulfill their potential and have the resiliency to meet life's challenges. This comprehensive book covers every area of self-esteem, and shows educators how to nurture it in the schoolplace." **Dr. Masa Goetz, Psychologist**

"Children must feel worthy in order to value their worth; must feel confident in order to assert themselves; and must feel competent in order to feel confident. Instilling a positive self-esteem in your students may be the single most important thing that you bestow. How to teach it is the eloquently presented subject of: *The 6 Vital Ingredients*, a 'must read' for all educators seeking to accomplish this momentous goal." **Dr. Terry Stimson, Educator and Former Senator, Alaska**

"With impressive insights and practical applications, this beautifully written book furnishes educators with the tools to develop positive self-esteem in students, while also providing them with information detailing its importance." **Dr. Pat Hould, Principal, Thompson Falls, Montana**

"Probably no one characteristic will guarantee our student's success in life more than possessing a healthy self-esteem. Dr. Youngs' book provides us with practical information on how we can develop this all-important sense of self in our students. A must for anyone working with youth!" **Dr. Thomas Drake, Principal, Lincoln High School, Des Moines, Iowa**

"A valuable resource for effective parenting and teaching. Providing a positive, purposeful and loving environment can change the world. Dr. Maria Montessori, a noted 20th century educator said, 'Let the child always experience success before failure.' Definitely a book all educators must read. **Barbara Moffit, Editor of the *Reporter*, the quarterly Journal of the National Center for Montessori Education**

"Whether making new friends, taking a spelling test, or getting a part-time job, a child's success is influenced by his inner view of self. This book offers step-by-step instructions and advice on how to make certain that youth develop it." **Dr. Bob Love, Sitka, Alaska**

"This comprehensive and compassionate book provides us with the knowledge to ensure that our students meet life equipped with a positive view of themselves and their abilities necessary in order to prosper in the world." **Martha Posey, Lake Mary High School, Florida**

"Nothing is more important than a healthy self-esteem in assuring that our children become happy and productive adults; perhaps no one else is more qualified to provide us with the knowledge and instruction necessary in order to bring about this level of self-esteem in our nation's youth than Bettie. I've had the opportunity to watch Bettie Youngs as a parent and educator over the years. Her message works!" **Dr. Lynn Fox, Professor of Education, San Francisco State University**

"This wonderful book shows you how to raise self-esteem in children, to assure that they are loaded with self-confidence. Every parent and educator should read and re-read this important book." **Brian Tracy, Brian Tracy Learning Systems**

"From goal setting, to confidence-building and role-playing, Dr. Youngs' book furnishes us with the tools for building self-esteem in youth, and a wealth of information and instruction on how to achieve this crucial objective." **Bill McGrane, National Self-Esteem Institute, Cincinnati, Ohio**

"The 6 Vital Ingredients of Self-Esteem: physical safety, emotional security, identity, belonging, competence and purpose, are thoroughly addressed in Dr. Youngs' impressive and timely book. I wholeheartedly recommend it." **David Jones, Brantford Collegiate, Canada**

"A parent can have no more noble aspiration than to help her child decide that he is a winner. One should not forget, however, that the parent and educator who reads and applies this wisdom to his child-rearing consequently benefits as well." **Dee Carlson, Educator and Parent, Fossil, Oregon**

"When we talk about *developing potential*, we're talking about helping a child develop self-esteem. This book is a *powerful* tool in the hands of any educator (or parent) who applies its insights, wisdom and instruction." **Shelly Hungerford, PTA, Burbank, CA**

"Self-esteem is the key, opening countless doors for the child who has the benefit of its possession. This should be required reading for educators, and administrators." **Egil Hjertaker, Norwegian Society for Humanistic Education and Psychology, Oslo, Norway**

"Life is filled with numerous obstacles and challenges. Making certain that our children are equipped to face those challenges and cope with those obstacles is part of our responsibility as educators. Developing high self-esteem is perhaps the most important tool for such coping. Dr. Youngs' vital book teaches us how to empower youth with this essential sense of self." **Dr. Ann Swain, Principal, Platte Valley School District, Colorado**

"The 6 Vital Ingredients of Self-Esteem supplies us with information, instruction and insights on building self-esteem in youth. With so many demands on their judgment and morals today, providing our children with this level of self-esteem is of vital importance. All educators and parents will find Dr. Youngs' book enormously helpful because it provides answers with common sense advice and practical instruction." **Dr. Len Trisch, Oregon State Department of Education**

"Secure, self-accepting, cheerful, confident, a positive attitude — who wouldn't want these attributes, the benefits of high self-esteem, for youth? How to build and develop this level of self-esteem is covered in detail in this rich and nourishing book. Dr. Youngs' book outfits us with the knowledge and understanding to begin and continue this ongoing mission of priority." **Dr. Jan Gooding, Alma, Michigan**

"A composite of 6 vital ingredients at work, self-esteem is immeasurably important to our children's present and future. Dr. Youngs' book describes these 6 ingredients in detail, and teaches us how to develop this crucial level of self-esteem in youth." **Dr. Doris Okada, California State University**

"Helping youth make and sustain friends, find meaning in life, build competence and confidence, feel safe and emotionally secure — all this is included in Dr. Youngs' invaluable book; and all this is part and parcel to developing high self-esteem in children. We can all benefit from reading and applying the knowledge this volume imparts." **William Ybarra, Los Angeles County Office of Education**

"We know that self-image and esteem affects performance and achievement. Dr. Youngs' book shows us how to instill confidence, and help youth feel capable. This book is an important source of practical information and instruction on building our students' self-esteem." **Dr. Patricia Fitzmorris, San Diego County Office of Education**

"The child with a good self-esteem has the best chance of being a happy and successful adult. Self-esteem is the armor that protects kids from the dragons of life: drugs, alcohol, unhealthy relationships, and delinquency." **Dr. Ken Robb, Superintendent of Schools, Ontario, Canada**

"Few things could be more important than the possession of high self-esteem in assuring that children become happy and productive adults; few books could be better equipped to provide educators with the knowledge and instruction necessary in order to bring about this level of self-esteem in students." **Dr. George R. Gibbs, Assistant Superintendent, Alma Public Schools, Michigan**

"Comprehensive in content — from goal setting, to confidence-building and role-playing — Dr. Youngs' book furnishes exercises for building self-esteem in students, as well as supplying a wealth of additional information and instruction on how to achieve this crucial objective in the young people we educators work with and influence." **Dr. Jack Hill, Superintendent of Schools, Imperial Valley, CA**

"Teaching your students that you value and respect them may be the single most important lesson any educator can teach since it helps youth to value and respect themselves — a major part of acquiring high self-esteem. How to teach that value and respect is presented in the eloquent and realistic text of Dr. Youngs' book, a 'must read' for all who seek to accomplish this worthy goal." **Mary Louise Martin, Principal, Central Elementary, San Diego City Schools, San Diego, CA**

"Certainly an educator can aspire to few things that are more noble than to help each student decide that he is capable. I was duly impressed with Dr. Youngs' book which teaches how to accomplish just such assistance in building high self-esteem. Without a doubt, this book will benefit any educator who reads and applies its wisdom and thus benefit their students as well." **Dr. Rita King, California Department of Education, Sacramento, CA**

"This book is a powerful tool in the hands of any educator who applies its insight, wisdom, and instruction to his or her classroom skills. I challenge all educators to take the time to read it, and to begin applying its wealth of instruction." **Dr. Pat Cole, Assistant Superintendent of Education, Wyandotte, Michigan**

"I am most eager to implement the *6 Vital Ingredients of Self-Esteem* in my Montessori Center. You have shown me how to assist children to meet challenge head-on, to be responsible, productive, and creative. As Aristotle stated over two thousand years ago, 'Happiness is self-contentedness.'" **Nancy Terry Sager, Founder and Director, Santa Fe Montessori School, Solana Beach, CA**

"This book is an empowering resource on building self-esteem in students. In order to value their worth, children must *feel* worthy; in order to do well in school, they must feel confident academically. This means they must posses a high self-esteem. Developing that level of self-esteem is addressed in this enlightening and pragmatic book." **Dr. Billie Jean Knight, Principal, Manhattan Beach City School District, Manhattan Beach, CA**

TABLE OF CONTENTS

6. EMOTIONAL SECURITY:
Dealing with Students' Fears and Insecurities

7. IDENTITY:
Helping Students Answer the "WHO AM I?" Question

8. IDENTITY:
A Student's Search for Self

9. AFFILIATION:
The Student's Need for Adult Friendships

14. BECOMING AN EFFECTIVE EDUCATOR:
Developing Your Educational Philosophy

15. TAKING ON THE CHALLENGE:
Putting Self-Esteem on Your Agenda

Chapter 1

UNLEASHING THE WILL TO LEARN:
The Effect of Self-Esteem on Learning

What we want to see is the child in pursuit of knowledge and not knowledge in pursuit of the child. — *George Bernard Shaw*

Catherine looked around her classroom, searching the faces of her seventh grade students. She was dismayed to see several students staring off into space, while others doodled or flipped idly through their textbooks. A few students met her gaze, but Catherine didn't see the spark of anticipation in their eyes that should have been there. Yet Catherine had worked hard to make this lesson interesting and meaningful for her students. Why did it seem that each year fewer and fewer students were curious learners? Was it her imagination, or were more and more students uninterested in exploring, discovering, questing? "Why is it so difficult to motivate these young people?" Catherine asked herself. "Why won't Ronny attempt to do better? I know he can. What makes Holly always seem so sad? Why doesn't Suzanne understand that she is a very capable student? If she'd only try!"

If you've had days like Catherine's, when it seems impossible to unleash the will to learn in your students, then perhaps you've asked yourself some of these questions:

- How can I get her to feel better about herself?
- How can I get him to lead from his strengths instead of focusing on the negative?
- How can I have him choose a goal that will excite and motivate him?
- How can I help her show respect and gain acceptance from her classmates?
- How can I get him to be responsible for his actions?

As an educator in today's school system, you may grapple with these questions more than you have in the past. If it seems to you that fewer of your students have an inner sense of self-confidence, a drive to set and achieve goals, or a desire to be successful, you are not alone. Like you, I see more and more students like Ronny or Holly or Suzanne. A Colorado superintendent best summed it up when he said, "I have the most dedicated, competent, and professional staff I've ever worked with. Our curriculum is aligned with state frameworks, our materials are up to par, and we have special services designed to meet the needs of our youth. But the gap between meeting our goals and meeting the needs of our students is wider than ever. Parents are sending us the wrong kids!"

Today's students need so much. Our students are besieged on all sides. Statistics show that in the United States, every year, nearly 37% of all students drop out of school; nearly one million children run away from home; one out of 10 teens becomes pregnant, and one out of seven students deals with the trauma of parents divorcing, some for the second time. Combine those grim statistics with the fact that more than 30% of today's young people are involved with substance abuse, and you have an equation of stress, pain, and suffering that touches almost every student in your classroom. No wonder so many students are uncertain about themselves and their future. No wonder they are unaware of how much positive potential resides within themselves. And no wonder that so many students seem so afraid of confronting yet another failure that they won't risk putting themselves on the line to excel or achieve goals. Factors such as dropping out, pregnancy, and substance abuse all lower motivation and erode self-esteem. It's a vicious cycle — low self-esteem results in lowered motivation, low motivation prevents students from becoming efficient and effective learners.

Low self-esteem creates a vicious cycle.

Self-esteem. We hear the word a lot these days, but what is it really? What detracts from or empowers self-esteem? How is self-esteem developed in the childhood (K-12) years? How is self-esteem enhanced or eroded in the schoolplace? What is the relationship between self-esteem and motivation? What specific actions can educators take to build positive self-esteem in their students? How does the possession of a high self-esteem relate to setting and achieving purposeful goals? What is self-esteem's contribution to the development of a sense of responsibility for individual well-being and, on a larger scale, social responsibility? What is the relationship between a positive self-esteem and inner happiness? How does self-esteem contribute to our ability to attract healthy and mutual relationships? How does self-esteem help us to become, as Carl Rogers said, "fully functioning persons"? What is self-esteem's role in helping us become what Abraham Maslow, the famous psychologist from Brandeis University, called the "self-actualizing person" and the "fully human person"?

These are big questions and important ones. Looking to the value of self-esteem as having a role in answering these questions is a step in the right direction. Self-esteem is central to what we make of our lives — the loyalty we have to developing ourselves and to caring about others. Self-esteem is at the heart of what we will achieve in the course of our lifetime. Nothing affects health and energy, peace of mind, the goals we set and achieve, our inner happiness, the quality of our relationships, our competence, performance, and our productivity quite so much as the health of our self-esteem.

With self-esteem being so important, educators need to know how to best use teaching time to help students develop a sense of self that will yield inner strength and motivation, create a desire to achieve and excel, and unleash potential — so that students will want to create for themselves a rewarding and purposeful life. As educators, we can and must encourage self-esteem in the schoolplace.

We do this by creating an environment that supports and reinforces the practices that strengthen self-esteem. This is one of the most important things we do.

Self-Esteem: A Definition

Self-esteem is self-regard. It is the esteem you hold for you, the value you place on your personhood. Self-esteem is a composite picture of *self-value.*

Author and psychologist Nathaniel Branden, perhaps the father of modern self-esteem philosophy, explains that self-esteem is the intergrated sum of self-efficacy and self-respect.[1] **Self-efficacy** is defined as having confidence in your ability to think, judge, choose, and decide. It's knowing and understanding your interests and needs. It incorporates self-trust and self-reliance. The experience of self-efficacy generates a sense of control over your life, a sense of being at the vital center of your existence — not just a passive spectator and a victim of events. **Self-respect** is defined as having confidence in your values. It's an affirmative attitude toward the right to live and be happy, and to have the freedom to assert your thoughts, wants, needs, and joys. Self-respect allows for mutual regard of others and makes possible a non-neurotic sense of fellowship.

> Self-esteem is self-regard...it is a composite picture of self-value.

Self-efficacy and self-respect are the dual pillars of healthy self-esteem. If either one is absent, self-esteem is impaired.

Branden explains it this way: "Consider that if an individual felt inadequate to face the challenges of life, if an individual lacked fundamental self-trust, confidence in his or her mind, we would recognize the presence of a self-esteem deficiency, no matter what other assets he or she possessed. Or if an individual lacked a basic sense of self-respect, felt unworthy, or undeserving of the love or respect of others, unentitled to happiness, fearful of asserting thoughts, wants, or needs — again we would recognize a self-esttem deficiency, no matter what other positive attributes he or she exhibited."

The correlation between a student's self-esteem and his level of confidence, between self-esteem and achievement, between self-esteem and risk-taking, between self-esteem and goal attainment is well documented. Coopersmith's[2] historical and ground-breaking research gave us a framework for understanding the importance of self-esteem, and Reasoner's[3] work added belonging and purpose as critical elements to self-esteem development. Borba[4] connected each element to curriculum content. Other experts, including The National Council for Self-Esteem, champion its important contribution to developing personal and social responsibility. Building on these foundations, my work with educators, youth, and parents over the years has led me to believe that there are six vital areas that contribute to or detract from the level of a student's self-esteem. Positive experi-

[1]Nathaniel Branden. *Psychology of Self-Esteem.* Los Angeles: Bantam Books, Nash Publishing Co., 1969.

[2]Stanley Coopersmith. *The Antecedents of Self-Esteem.* San Francisco, CA: W. H. Freeman, 1967.

[3]Robert Reasoner, and R. Gilbert. *Building Self-Esteem: Implementation Project Summary.*
ERIC Clearinghouse on Counseling and Personnel Services #CG 029089, 1988.

[4]Michele Borba. *Esteem Builders.* Rolling Hills Estates, CA: Jalmar Press, 1989.

ences in these six areas serve to build a positive sense of self, while negative experiences in one or more of these areas seriously erodes a child's self-esteem.

The six are:

> **Physical safety:** Freedom from physical harm.
> **Emotional security:** The absence of intimidations and fears.
> **Identity:** The "Who am I?" question.
> **Affiliation:** A sense of belonging.
> **Competence:** A sense of feeling capable.
> **Mission:** The feeling that one's life has meaning and direction.

The overall health of your self-esteem can render you psychologically hardy or vulnerable, capable or incapable, vivacious or despondent. This is why you might think a particular student has everything going for him but inside *he* may not see the same picture. If you've ever looked at a student and thought, "If only Jane had any idea how capable she is! If only Tom knew how bright he is!" then you get the idea. While your view and the student's view differ, he acts on his inner picture. Self-esteem, then, is a consequence. It's your total "score" or *value*. This score becomes your price tag, so to speak. Self-esteem is the way *you* see yourself. It is very personal.

A person with high self-esteem may see himself as "top-of-the-line merchandise," while the low self-esteem person may view himself as "damaged goods." Today it seems that more and more children view themselves as "damaged goods." The effects of low self-esteem make it difficult for our children to rise up to tackle the challenges and opportunities of life.

All Individuals Want and Need to Matter

We all need to feel worthwhile, valuable, and purposeful. This is as true for children as it is for adults. We each need to know that we are giving our time — the substance of our life — to something special. That's why teaching can be enormously fulfilling when we feel that we are making a difference, or it can be unrewarding when we feel that we aren't, just as being a student can either be emotionally satisfying or desperately trying. When we feel that we don't matter — when we are squandering time (life) — the esteem we hold for our value is lessened. Such feelings erode self-esteem, making it harder for us to bounce back in the face of adversity in future endeavors.

Destructive behaviors are increasing among all students.

Perhaps you've noticed that there seems to be a great many more young people (and adults) at risk today. "At risk" is a common expression used by schools, social service agencies, and the criminal justice system to denote potential risk factors in those young people most likely to fall prey to destructive activities. Once, or so it seemed, only certain students were at risk for becoming involved in destructive behaviors. Not so today. When we don't pay attention to the emotional life or physical whereabouts of children, then all children are at risk. Destructive behaviors are increasing among all students — not just the ones we label as "at risk" because they are economically-deprived, or physically- or emotionally-abused. Many students are at risk these days. The attendant symptoms — drug involvement, youth pregnancy, dropping out of school, disrespect for educators, parents, and fellow students, and apathy and boredom, and other such maladies — show us just how much destruction young people can inflict upon themselves and others. With our educational system's increased focus on academics in the absence of attention to the important character-building principles — such as ethics, integrity, responsibility — we are likely to see continuing increase in destructive behavior.

Educators Are Really Important People!

Educators are *powerful, important* people. You *do* make a difference to your students. All children pass through the hands of educators. What educators do and say (and how they do and say it) *becomes the foundation on which many children will build their lives*. For some students, the positive environment in the schoolplace is the only positive aspect of their lives. *Many* children find solace in school because, for them, it's where some of the best things happen.

With the challenge of teaching in today's school system, it's often easy to forget how influential we are in our students' lives. Developing someone's potential is, as students say, an "awesome" responsibility. Inherent in the role of an educator is the ability to provide leadership and to empower our students. We do this by helping students believe in themselves. In a very real sense, a positive self-regard is the important and lasting legacy we bestow upon our students. We help them experience their essence and assign it purposeful value. We help youth feel that they matter, that they are worthwhile, that they can "believe, achieve, and succeed." We want them to know that they are the makers of their dreams and the creators of their realities.

Helping students believe that they possess the ability to discover their own reality and test its boundaries is an important contribution on our behalf. We do that by creating an environment where positive self-regard can flourish.

Teachers can create an environment where self-esteem can flourish.

Just Do It! We Can!

Teaching is both exhausting and exhilarating. It's big-time responsibility and hard work — much more so today than even a decade ago. But we are making gains. The more we know about children and the psychology of childhood, the more we research effective teaching methodologies, the more we discover about learning styles, and the more we test motivational theories in order to close the ever-increasing gap between what we want for our youth and their getting it, the more we are forced to look at the role of self-esteem in teaching and learning.

And that's good. If we're serious about developing healthy, happy, competent self-actualizing students, we must create a classroom environment where students can develop high self-esteem.

Where Should We Begin?

Unfortunately, students don't come with a parts and maintenance manual, although perhaps that's just as well — if they did, we'd have an overwhelming reading load! But even if you have 33 students going in 33 different directions, you can help them develop a healthy sense of self that will serve them now and in later years. **You can** learn to empower your students to meet life's challenges with confidence.

It begins with you. Seeing your students as winners helps convince them that they are winners, that they can do whatever they put to their minds to, and that they have to participate in the plan — the plan to become all they are capable of being.

Self-esteem is *really* that important. Enhancing the self-esteem of students is one of the most important roles of teaching.

Like Catherine, the teacher we met at the beginning of this chapter, I've always been interested in how we can equip our youth with the confidence and internal security they need to fully experience our world and to take an active role in it.

It's my goal in this book to provide a course of practical guidance in creating an environment that promotes positive self-esteem in our students. Chapters 1 through 3 of this book explore the way self-esteem affects us and how we can assess the levels of our students' self-esteem. Chapters 4 through 14 describe in detail the six vital ingredients of self-esteem and offer examples and exercises for teachers, students, and parents. Chapters 14 and 15 suggest ways to integrate self-esteem improvement with your individual teaching philosophy. Keep in mind that having high self-esteem does not a guarantee a happy, pain-free life, but if our self-esteem is high, we have the foundation we need to greet life with zest and zeal and to strive to achieve our full potential.

Chapter 2

YOUR SELF-ESTEEM IS SHOWING:
How Self-Esteem Influences Behavior

Self-esteem is a composite picture of key facets that determine how secure, complete, and whole you feel about yourself. Your self-worth is founded upon self-efficacy — an inner sense of confidence in your ability to live your life, secure that you can confront challenges, and self-respect — your willingness to stand up for yourself. The level of your self-esteem determines whether you feel worthy and deserving of having an *abundant* life, and all it entails.

Though self-esteem is your worth as *you* see it, others can easily discern it. Your actions are a direct reflection of your internal image of yourself. You wear your self-esteem. It shows! *Your outer actions are motivated by your inner sense of self.* As deeply personal as it is, the esteem you hold for yourself affects everything you do and say.

Just as for adults, our students' inner pictures influence the way they treat themselves and others. It affects how much they are liked and accepted by fellow students and how much they achieve. Have you ever looked at a student and thought that if only he felt better about himself, he would respond or behave differently? Conversely, did you come to realize that a student was over-achieving primarily because his image was one of being capable? A student's behavior is influenced by his feelings of worth and value. His behavior is a tell-tale sign of how he feels about himself.

Low self-esteem impairs our ability to function in healthy and appropriate ways. Dropping out of school, early pregnancy, drug abuse, and other destructive behaviors are linked to a student's self-esteem. For example, students who drop out of school often see little purpose to their lives. They may have a difficult time relating school success to the outside world, thus they see few reasons to improve themselves. Often they have difficulty developing warm relationships with peers and teachers — the support system that makes school a fun and endurable place. The inappropriate behaviors and self-destructive actions of these students are almost certainly a reflection of the negative picture they hold about themselves.

Low self-esteem impairs our ability to function in healthy ways.

Do You Park Beside Jalopies?

Have you ever pulled into a parking space, looked over, took note of the car you parked beside, and immediately made a judgment as to whether to stay there or look around for a different space? Maybe you were parked very close to the car, but decided the driver would take care not to ding your car, or perhaps you moved your car over enough so that when the driver of the other car opened his door, it wouldn't come into contact with your car. Either way, what principle governed your actions — why did you do that? Was it because you knew that the driver would treat your car as he did his own? If his car appeared unkept, you instinctively knew that it was unlikely that he would be cautious of your car. If he appeared to be careful with his possession, you deduced he would be careful with yours, too.

The essence of self-esteem is similar to this. How you feel about yourself determines not only how you take care of yourself, but the way you treat others. I know of children and adults who possess a whole and healthy sense of self, and I know others who have very little to lose. The degree to which you take responsibility for yourself and your actions is dependent upon your self-esteem, which in turn contributes to empowering self-esteem.

Parents and educators share the responsibility to help children.

Unless mentally impaired, adults shoulder the responsibility for the realities of their lives. We are responsible for how we care for ourselves, and how we allow others to treat us. But children are recipients of what adults have brought about for them. While many factors influence the development of a healthy sense of self-esteem, parents and educators share the responsibility to help children achieve the six vital ingredients of self-esteem. Throughout childhood, the six ingredients of self-esteem are acted upon for children largely by parents and educators. This book focuses on what each ingredient means and what you can do to empower your students, but in a nutshell, these ingredients are as follows:

The 6 Facets of Self-Esteem

A sense of physical safety: A child who feels physically safe isn't fearful of being harmed or hurt. Because he feels safe, he learns to be open and to trust others. He freely exercises a curious nature, which contributes to learning. He moves about with a sense of healthy assuredness. His body posture displays confidence. His tone of voice is hearty and he maintains eye contact when he's talking with you.

A sense of emotional security: A child develops a high level of emotional security when he knows he won't be put down or made to feel less worthy, or be emotionally beat up with sarcasm or hurtful words. Because he feels emotionally secure, he learns to be caring and compassionate with himself and others. He feels secure in sharing his opinions and ideas. He is respectful and considerate. He is outgoing and friendly. Because others have shown value for his self-regard, he is able to give himself positive and encouraging messages.

A sense of identity: A child with self-knowledge develops a healthy sense of individuality. He knows himself. He has made friends with the face in the mirror. He believes in his worth as a human being. He believes he is special and worthy of praise. Feeling secure about himself, he feels secure in praising and complimenting others.

A sense of affiliation: A student who feels accepted by and connected to others feels liked, appreciated, and respected. He learns to seek out and maintain friendships. He is able to cooperate and share. Feeling accepted and liked, he respects and shows acceptance of others. While maintaining a sense of independence, he learns *inter*dependence — a healthy perception of interrelatedness.

A sense of competence: When a student believes he is good at some things, he's willing to learn how to do other things. Because he feels capable, he perseveres rather than quits when things become difficult. Not only is he aware of his strengths, he accepts the areas where he's less competent, and does so without developing "victim" behavior. He takes responsibility for his actions, and owns up to them. Because he tries, he experiences the successes that encourage him to try new things. He is self-empowered through realistic and achievable goals.

A sense of mission: A student with a strong sense of mission feels purposeful. Life has meaning and direction. He sets goals and follows through on achieving them. When faced with obstacles, he generates creative alternatives. He has an inner knowledge, an inner peace. He is intuitive, he laughs easily, he is joyful. He makes his "toys his tools, his joys his job."

Self-esteem encompasses and expresses how valuable you feel *because* of what's going on in each of these six vital areas in your life. But these six areas are hierarchical and interdependent. Without a sense of physical safety, for example, a child cannot adequately perceive a sense of purpose. Once safety and emotional security are assured, the need for a sense of identity, belonging, competence, and purpose becomes important.

When these important areas are satisfactorily addressed, the student is more likely to see himself as capable and competent, loving and lovable, responsible and caring. You have "high self-esteem." Far from being conceited or self-centered, a healthy self-esteem gives you a realistic awareness of yourself and your abilities and needs. With an all-encompassing respect for yourself, you are unwilling to allow others to devalue your worth, nor will you let them deprive you of your needs.

From the first four ingredients — physical safety, emotional security, identity, and affiliation — children glean images of their worth through their relationships with parents and teachers and others with whom they spend considerable time. Here their self-esteem is a product of not only what they tell themselves, *but the messages from others about their worth as valuable persons*. In addition, children see how important they are *by our actions* toward them. This demonstrates whether we value them — actions do speak louder than words. The first four components of a child's self-esteem, especially in the first 16 years of his life, are regulated and manipulated by adults. We're largely responsible for the degree to which a young person develops his self-esteem.

In the other two areas of self-esteem, competence and purpose, the student's self-esteem is no longer solely dependent on the forces of others. These last two components expand a student's sense of herself and sets her empowerment cycle

These six areas are hierarchical and interdependent.

spinning in a forward motion. She begins to act on her own sense of what's important and what's not. Because she feels capable, she's willing to get involved. Setting goals and achieving them is *her* desire. She feels purposeful — her life has meaning and direction. She sets other goals for herself, creating a cycle of success. Each successful completion provides an internal validation that "I am a 'can do' individual." Even attempts have merit, sending an "I'm worthwhile" message to the student.

All Students Need a Healthy Self-Esteem

Positive self-esteem is essential for *all* children to develop and grow in a healthy way. This is true for high or low IQ students, for gifted or mentally disabled students, for athletic or physically disabled students, for good or poor students. Positive self-esteem is necessary for the student you like, and most especially, for the student you find it more difficult to like and to teach.

Everyone has a need to feel unafraid, secure, connected, capable, and competent. Children have an especially strong need to feel these things with their parents, teachers, and others who are a part of their lives. *All* students need a sense of worth and a feeling of "okay" in situations that are new and frightening to them as they learn, grow, and change through the K-12 years.

Characteristics of High Self-Esteem Students

Motivation and productivity skyrocket when students reach their goals.

What separates high self-esteem students from low self-esteem students is a "can-do" attitude. By focusing on their strengths and achievements, high self-esteem students accept mistakes and weaknesses without undue self-devaluation. Like adults, when children have a reserve of positive experiences to call on during tough times, they're better able to persist on their chosen course. Motivation and productivity skyrocket when these students reach their goals. They don't depend solely on others for approval, and are able to say to themselves, "I did it!" "I did a good job!" "I can do even better!" "That was great!" "That was fun!"

Building your students' self-esteem can create tremendous benefits. Students with high self-esteem exhibit characteristics that will serve them well in their daily work, as well as in later life. High self-esteem aids students in attaining the most from their lives:

■ The higher a student's self-esteem, the more psychological hardiness he brings to coping with adversity and diversity.

■ The higher a student's self-esteem, the greater zest, zeal, and gusto he brings to the treatment of his experiences, the more ambitious he will be in setting and achieving goals that are purposeful.

■ The higher a student's self-esteem, the better able he is to develop and sustain nourishing relationships.

■ The higher a student's self-esteem, the better able he will be to attract others who enjoy their lives and are working to their potential. Individuals with low self-esteem tend to seek low self-esteem peers who think poorly of themselves.

■ Students with high self-esteem are more secure confronting obstacles, fears, and interpersonal conflicts. High self-esteem helps students to solve problems instead of worrying over them. Low self-esteem students see problems as grounds for quitting, and often say to themselves, "I give up." Instead of comparing their achievements with their own goals and potential, students with low self-esteem compare themselves with others, and wait for others to create "successes" for them.

■ Students with high self-esteem find better ways to get along well with others and respond positively to them. Students with high self-esteem strive to be useful, helpful, purposeful, and responsible.

■ Students with high self-esteem are more compassionate toward themselves and others. Compassion increases self-worth and enables the student to *discover the treasured value of his selfhood*.

■ Students with high self-esteem are more secure, decisive, friendly, trusting, cheerful, optimistic, and purposeful. High self-esteem empowers and motivates. Students with high self-esteem recognize their own worth and achievements without a constant need for outside approval. This does not mean that they don't need others, but rather, that they are *inter*-dependent (versus *de*pendent) on others. Low self-esteem students are usually described as moody, aloof, fearful, aimless, negative, and indecisive. Look closely and you'll note that these students need constant reinforcement from others, and use attention-getting antics to meet their needs of self-worth.

Students with high self-esteem are more secure, decisive, and purposeful.

■ Students with high self-esteem take more responsibility and control over their actions. This is important not only because students who monitor their own actions are responsible, but because these students are more willing to accept challenges and extend their boundaries *because* they have experienced previous successes. Recognition of personal strengths and capabilities serves as a powerful strategy for overcoming obstacles, and helps compensate for weaknesses and setbacks. Obviously, these students have met with their share of failure, but they focus on their positive experiences.

When we instill realistic confidence in the minds of our students, and help them to feel secure within themselves, they are more likely to respond appropriately to the challenges and opportunities that lie before them.

Discussion

1. How does self-esteem manifest itself in children? Think of students you know with high and low self-esteem.

2. Why is self-esteem important to students? When do they begin to form a sense of self-esteem?

3. Is the classroom an appropriate place to discuss self-esteem? Is building self-esteem part of the educator's job, or is it a parent's responsibility?

Exercise

1. Go back over this chapter and summarize the benefits of encouraging a positive sense of self-regard in students. Discuss it with other staff members. Decide on a plan of action to enhance self-esteem in all students. What will be done at the classroom level? What will be done at the school climate level? How will all school personnel — from the office staff to the bus drivers — participate in the plan?

2. Write a letter on the importance of self-esteem to send home to parents, listing practical things they can do to enhance their children's self-esteem.

Chapter 3

SELF-ESTEEM IS THE FINAL SCORE:
Assessing Self-Esteem in Students

How can you tell whether a student has a healthy sense of self or not? You can't always assume that the quiet, shy or "D-" student has a low self-esteem, while the outgoing, rambunctious, popular or "A" student has a high self-esteem. There's more to it than that. Here are some guidelines to help you make a better assessment.

Indications of High Self-Esteem

■ **Willingness to participate.** Students with high self-esteem are willing, even eager, to join in. They are secure in their ability to succeed, or at least to have fun trying. Observe your students. When a student is invited to participate in an activity or group, how does he or she respond? For example, does the student want to try out for a school team or belong to an organization or club? Does he look forward to the fun of being together with classmates at school outings, special events or sports functions? When asked to join a group of classmates for a project, or participate in a discussion, does he willingly do so? Or is he reluctant to participate in just about everything?

Students with a healthy self-esteem often participate joyfully in a number and range of experiences. They feel they have something to offer. They aren't bogged down with the notion that they have to excel at everything in order to participate, nor are they worried that others will poke fun at them if they aren't good at it. They have curiosity, a desire to experiment, and a natural willingness to be with others.

■ **Willingness to share.** Most young people enjoy talking about themselves and their interests. We call this *self-disclosure*. Students with self-knowledge and an appreciation of themselves are not shy about passing along compliments or the praise others have given them. This sharing is healthy and normal. Talking about successes doesn't necessarily denote an unhealthy ego. It indicates a sense of comfort and self-acceptance. And, students who accept compliments from others are more willing to compliment and praise others in return. Often, they are the first to say, "You got an A, awwwright, you're a cool dude!"

■ **Ability to accept advice without viewing it as criticism.** When students have high self-esteem, they accept advice without viewing it as criticism. Constructive feedback is received with an attitude of acceptance. Such students are willing

> Students with a healthy self-esteem are secure in their ability to succeed.

to admit when they are wrong or have made a mistake, and self-correct. Low self-esteem students often view advice as criticism, and take criticism as a form of rejection. Fear of rejection prompts them to avoid admitting when they are wrong or have made a mistake. They may lie or cheat to cover up their misgivings.

Being one of the crowd is a normal, important desire.

■ **Comfort with themselves.** Students with healthy self-esteem do not have to always be surrounded by classmates or friends. They are happy with their own company. They don't always have to "find themselves" or define themselves through the opinions of others. Being one of the crowd — peer acceptance — is a normal, important desire, but young people with a positive sense of self-regard can be with others without excessively depending on them.

■ **Commitment to achieving.** Students with a healthy self-esteem want to do well, and aren't intimidated by tackling the challenge of understanding something they don't yet comprehend. These students generally compete with themselves rather than with others. They might boast about their improvements or even engage in some healthy competition with friends and offer up good-natured teasing ("I got two more right than you did!" "I can run faster than you can!" "I bet I can beat you at . . ."), but it's done with a good-hearted spirit. Through it all, they are comfortable with themselves and aren't desperate to be better than absolutely everyone else. Students with low self-esteem are poor sports anytime someone does something better than they can.

Indications of Low Self-Esteem

The signs indicating low self-esteem may take diametrically opposite forms, manifesting themselves in behavioral problems, in demanding constant attention, or in complete withdrawal. Some general warning signs include:

■ **Negative behavior.** A belligerent student, one who intentionally repeats negative behavior, may be showing you how little she respects herself. She may comment about how "dumb" school is, or how "stupid" the assignments are, and so on. She constantly goads you, looking for "proof" to convince herself that she really is unworthy and unlovable.

■ **Constant self-belittling.** Students who *always* make "I can't" or "I'm not" statements or other self-defeating remarks have low opinions of themselves. All students make comments of this sort on occasion; it's time for concern when these put-downs become a frequent part of their communications.

■ **Admiration without emulation.** If a student talks about his heroes or friends but never makes an attempt to emulate them, it might be because he feels he can never be as good as those heroes or friends. For example, a girl might copy an admired friend's hairstyle. If she has a healthy sense of self-esteem, she does so because she believes she has the capability to accomplish what she wants, and a willingness to try something new. If she constantly says things such as, "Everybody likes Amanda but nobody likes me. No one *ever* likes me," she lacks the self-confidence and self-esteem to risk making and sustaining friendships.

■ **Lack of caring about attention from you.** All students want their teachers to notice their accomplishments. Even teens who feel they are fatally misunderstood and who think adults are hopelessly outdated occasionally seek your approval, in a casual, off-handed way. It's time for concern when a student no longer seeks your approval at all, or no longer bothers trying to get your attention, or when it seems she doesn't care about your feelings toward her.

■ **Excessive criticism of others.** When a student constantly criticizes you and others, he may lack confidence in himself. In order to build himself up, he believes he must belittle those around him. Although he may not be conscious of it, this is his way of trying to feel superior.

■ **Excessive concern with the attention and opinions of peers.** Students who place tantamount importance on the opinions and attention of friends rarely assert their judgment when faced with the disapproval of their peers. Because these students don't trust their own ideas and thoughts, they take on the thoughts, values, and actions of others, even when they know in their own hearts that those actions are contrary to what they want or to what they know is right.

How Well Do You Know Your Students?

As an effective and caring educator, you make a point of talking with your students in order to get to know them as individuals. You observe their actions, overhear their conversations, and feel you understand at least a little bit about what makes each one tick. Yet, you may be surprised to know how differently students see themselves. To help students build their self-esteem, you need to know how your students are faring in each of these six vital areas of self-esteem. The following assessment tool, designed for students themselves, can help you do that. You may duplicate the following self-esteem fitness profile for your students. The directions to the student on how to complete the assessment, as well as scoring of this instrument, are self-explanatory.

All students want their teachers to notice their accomplishments.

EXERCISE ONE

THE SELF-ESTEEM FITNESS PROFILE FOR YOUNG ADULTS
© 1991 Bettie B. Youngs, Ph.D.

Maybe you haven't spent too much time thinking about your self-esteem, but it's important that you do. Just like you need to care for your physical body, you need to know if your self-esteem is healthy and fit. Is your self-esteem working for you or against you? The following assessment can help you decide. It's designed to help you examine six key areas in your life and the experiences in each that account for how you feel about yourself. Keep in mind this is not a test; there are no "right" or "wrong" answers — no high or low scores. This is an opportunity for you to get to know yourself a little better.

Read each of the following statements, then circle **T** for true or **F** for false to indicate whether this is an accurate or inaccurate description of yourself. Don't think about each statement too long, or try to analyze it. Just go with your first response. Answer each question based on how you feel most of the time, not on how you feel during particularly good or bad days. This exercise will take about 15 minutes to complete.

> **EXAMPLE:** I get nervous when I have to give a report in front of the class.

> If you get nervous when you have to give a report in front of the class, circle **T** for true.

> If you do not get nervous when you have to give a report in front of the class, circle **F** for false.

PHYSICAL SAFETY

T F   1. I like the neighborhood I live in; I feel safe there.
T F   2. I like my home, and always feel safe there.
T F   3. I like the school I go to; I always feel safe there.
T F   4. I'm not afraid of any student at school.
T F   5. I seldom go to the nurse's office because of a headache or stomachache.
T F   6. I always make wise choices for the health of my body.
T F   7. I have a healthy, strong, and fit body.
T F   8. My parents discipline fairly.
T F   9. I feel safe in each of my classes.
T F   10. I'm not afraid of anyone in my neighborhood.

EMOTIONAL SECURITY

   T   F   1. I am a self-confident person.

   T   F   2. I am able to laugh at my own mistakes.

   T   F   3. It helps to talk about my feelings.

   T   F   4. I am my own best friend.

   T   F   5. I expect good things to happen to me.

   T   F   6. When I mess up, I just try to do it right the next time.

   T   F   7. I give myself credit when I do something well.

   T   F   8. I do not think it's important to do everything well.

   T   F   9. I try never to make fun of others and tease them unfairly.

   T   F 10. I know how to deal with stress and pressure.

SELFHOOD, IDENTITY

   T   F   1. I am a happy person.

   T   F   2. I seldom wish I could be someone else.

   T   F   3. I like the way I look.

   T   F   4. I like who I am.

   T   F   5. I like my body.

   T   F   6. I rarely think that if I had more money and things (like new CDs or more clothes) I would be a lot happier and have more friends.

   T   F   7. I take care of my appearance, trying to look my best every day.

   T   F   8. When something good happens to me, I feel I deserve it.

   T   F   9. I feel comfortable in most situations, even new ones.

   T   F 10. I often compliment others.

AFFILIATION, BELONGING

   T   F   1. I have at least two best friends.

   T   F   2. Other people are willing to help me when I need it.

   T   F   3. Whenever I say I will do something, people know I can be counted on.

   T   F   4. When good things happen to my friends, I'm happy for them.

   T   F   5. I like most of the people I know, even if we aren't good friends.

   T   F   6. I'm able to pal around with who I want: I can pick and choose my friends.

   T   F   7. Not all my friends are like me.

   T   F   8. I'm not intimidated by those who tease me and make fun of me.

T F   9. My friends know they can count on me for compliments
         when they have new clothes or have done something well.

T F   10. Others want to include me in what they are doing.

COMPETENCE

T F   1. I believe people who set goals get what they want out of life.

T F   2. I know how to set priorities and manage my time.

T F   3. I'm smart enough to do what I want when I put my mind to it.

T F   4. I ask others for help when I need it.

T F   5. I take my problems one step at a time.

T F   6. I can make wise choices and good decisions.

T F   7. I listen to the other person's point of view before I decide
         what to say.

T F   8. When I have trouble paying attention, I just refocus.

T F   9. I don't feel that I always have to do well in everything;
         sometimes giving it my best is enough.

T F   10. I feel capable of coping with life's challenges.

MISSION, PURPOSE

T F   1. I often think about my future and what it will be like.

T F   2. My life has meaning and direction.

T F   3. Whether I succeed or fail is up to me.

T F   4. I know that I'm going to get what I want out of life.

T F   5. I know what I want to do with my life.

T F   6. I've thought about what I want out of life.

T F   7. I am excited about my present life and look forward
         to my future.

T F   8. I've thought about what kind of a lifestyle I want to live.

T F   9. There are a lot of things I'm interested in.

T F   10. I have goals, and I'm going to achieve them.

SCORING

The best way to get an idea of your students' level of self-esteem is to look at each category separately. If a student has more than three negative responses in any single category, it's an area where he's feeling insecure, and one that can be eroding his self-esteem. An area that is low might signal a need for counseling. You might wish to hold a conference with his other teachers to see if they, too, have some concerns about his self-image and its effects on his behavior, performance, and achievement. You also might enlist the help of the school counselor and the support of this student's parents to fortify joint efforts in building his self-esteem.

You will want to also discuss the specific responses individually with the student. Does he feel insecure in a number of areas or just one or two? Did the student understand the directions? Has he learned to accept himself for who he is? Does he feel capable and in charge in most areas? Has he learned to accept responsibility for his actions?

EXERCISE TWO

This next exercise can help students specifically examine their day-to-day lives to see how events, some within their control, some wholly outside of it, can affect their self-esteem. Students need to understand that while they cannot always control what happens to them, they can control their reactions and not let it lower their self-esteem. The goal is to have students examine how the events of their day add to or detract from their self-esteem, and how the events of the day are somewhat less important than their response to these events. Duplicate the following pages and assist students in doing the exercise. If your students are in grades 1-3, redesign a similar exercise based on their abilities.

A note to teachers: The directions explain how to use the example scenario, but the best "stories" are those that happen in the lives of your students. You might want to have students write out the events of their own day — yesterday or any day that they can recall. Make a copy of the self-esteem charting grid for each student so they can chart the effects of events on their own self-esteem, or ask them to construct a personalized scoring sheet. Ask students to do this exercise regularly so they can see how daily events affect self-esteem over time.

STUDENT DIRECTIONS:

Read the statements that describe Amy's day. Using a 1-10 rating scale, 10 being highest, 1 being lowest, record a "score" after each statement to describe how you think it would affect her self-esteem that day. For example, if Amy washed her face and noticed that her complexion was clean and glowing that morning, her self-esteem would be high. If she noticed a new pimple, maybe she would feel self-conscious about herself. Some things do not have much of an effect on self-esteem. If Amy heard on the radio that the school her cousin attends had won a swim championship, she might not be affected at all, since she was not on the swim team and had no friends who were swimmers. The goal of this exercise is to help you think about how the little things that happen to you each day can make you feel good about yourself or how they make you feel bad. On the charting grid draw an X to indicate how you believe each event affected Amy's day. Next, connect the X's to get a picture of how these events affected Amy's day.

Amy's Day

a. Amy wakes up to her clock radio playing the song that she and her former boyfriend considered "their song." It's the one that was playing when they met.

b. As Amy brushes her hair, she can't do a thing with it. She is out of hairspray and mousse. She is certain her friends will tease her about the way she looks.

c. Amy washes her face and notices that her complexion is clean and glowing.

d. In school, Amy's best friend tells her that Michael, the most popular boy in school, said he thought Amy was cute but dumb.

e. Amy tells her friend how awesome her new jacket is and how good she looks in it. Her friend says, "Thanks, you always say the nicest things to me! If you ever want to borrow it, it's yours!"

f. During lunch, Michael waves at Amy.

g. In History class, Amy gets back her paper with a B+ and the comment, "You can do really good work when you put your mind to it; maybe the next paper will be an A!"

h. Amy gets called on in Math class and gives the wrong answer. She makes a joke out of her mistake and everyone laughs, including the teacher.

i. At volleyball practice after school, Amy gets a note from her best friend saying that she can't go to the school picnic with her this weekend because she and another friend are going to the amusement park with Michael and his friend.

j. That night Amy's sister brings home a report with an A+ on it. Amy's mom calls her mother to boast about the sister's work, but fails to mention that Amy has been selected as one of the five "Young Artists" in the city and that her art poster will be displayed in the convention center downtown.

k. Amy has no plans of being with friends this weekend and feels left out.

l. Amy's dog, Bart, senses that Amy is sad, so he hops up on her bed and curls up next to her.

m. Amy's dad comes in and says that he's really proud that she is his daughter and congratulates her on her being selected as a "Young Artist."

Now that you have completed this exercise, compare your responses with Amy's. How are they alike? How do they differ? Would you say that Amy's day had more of a positive or negative effect on her self-esteem?

CHARTING GRID

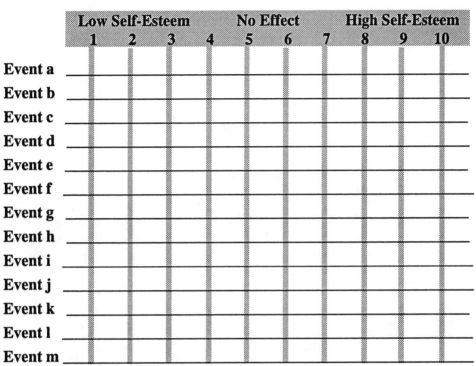

Here's how Amy filled out her grid.

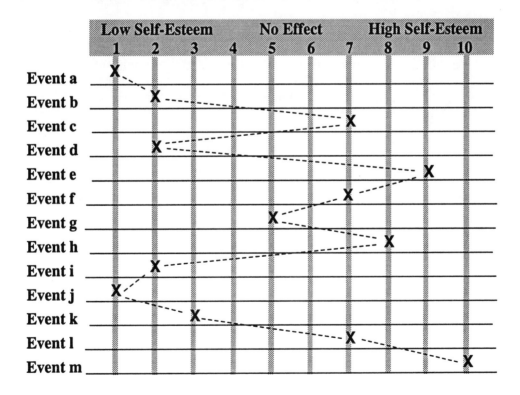

After your students have completed this alone, discuss it as a class. Again, there are no right or wrong answers. You may be surprised to find out how differently your students view these events. Some of the events are pretty straightforward. For example, having hair that "won't work" is very upsetting to most students. Even those with good self-esteem feel self-conscious and unhappy when they don't look like they want to look. Some of the statements are more ambiguous. How do your students think Amy would feel when she got a good grade, a B+, and praise from the teacher but then was told she could do even better? Would her self-esteem be raised because she had done well and because the teacher has confidence in her abilities, or would she be deflated because no matter how well she does she is always expected to do better? These questions lend themselves to good discussions.

High self-esteem is as important to a student as his reading level and test scores. A child benefits from instruction only if she considers herself capable and intelligent enough to learn. A "can-do" attitude makes taking on the challenge of learning possible.

High self-esteem is as important to a student as his reading level and test scores.

Discussion

1. How can you distinguish between a student with low self-esteem and one who is affected by temporary problems?

2. Can students hide low self-esteem by putting on a good act? How can you see through it?

3. Do you think students have an accurate idea of their friends' self-esteem? Can children identify low self-esteem in others and try to help them?

4. Can peer counseling help students with self-esteem issues?

Chapter 4

PHYSICAL SAFETY:
Is It Safe to Be in Your Classroom?

I've just boarded an American Airlines flight to New York City. "Welcome aboard flight 1547," says the stewardess. "Your safety is our number one priority." Safety. We all want to be free to move about our world without fear. Physical safety is the first in the **hierarchy** of the six vital ingredients of developing self-esteem. Physical safety is important because we need to be in control of our *self* in our environment — we need to have mastery over our being. An inner feeling of outer safety is a *prerequisite* needed before young people can progress to developing a healthy sense of self. Without physical safety, the development of a healthy self-esteem is severely limited. Only when students feel physically safe will they move beyond fear. Only then can students explore their day-to-day challenges in a naturally curious way.

Students who feel physically safe aren't fearful of being hurt in any way. When rules are in place to protect students, and when teachers show concern about their students' fears, students learn to trust. Because teachers and other school personnel can be counted on, students develop an increased sense of self-assuredness. But if students are fearful — for any reason — they tend to distrust others and shy away from them. Their fears make them uncomfortable in many situations, especially new or unfamiliar ones. Fearful students become defensive and are quick to judge others. Over time, they become angry, which causes them to lash out even more.

Hostility drives others further away, which increases the student's inner pain.

A downward circle is created: hostility, suspicion, and defensiveness drive others further away from the fearful student, which increases the student's inner pain. If you have ever confronted an angry or fearful student and yet have not known the cause of his or her negative feelings, consider this student's defensiveness a plea for your help.

How do fears take root and grow? While there are many causes, the lack of physical safety is a major factor that fuels a student's fears. Too many of our students suffer from emotional and physical neglect. Such suffering is not only shameful, it is inexcusable. And it is our children who pay the ultimate price as they learn only to inflict their suffering on others in a futile attempt to ease their own pain. Should it surprise us, then, that the absence of the most basic human needs results in a decrease of caring and nurturing, and an increase of apathy, general decay in the schoolplace, and violence inflicted by children against other children?

Why Some Children Fear Going to School

Not all schools provide a *safe* environment. Sadly, student violence escalates every year. Verbal and physical threats, assaults, injury, theft, arson, and vandalism are common. According to a safe school study of American schools, statistics show that in a typical month, 282,000 students were physically attacked; 112,000 students were robbed by someone using weapons or threats; 2.4 million students had personal property stolen; 800,000 students stayed home from school because they were afraid to attend; 2,400 fires were set in schools; and 1,000 teachers were assaulted seriously enough to require medical attention. Is it any wonder so many children (and more and more teachers) are frightened?

Student safety should be your school's No. 1 concern. It should also be your first concern in the classroom. Until a student feels physically safe, he will not be ready to meet the challenges of learning with the normal curiosity and excitement of an emotionally healthy and high self-esteem child. Although feeling safe doesn't guarantee that a child will be a learner, he can't be a learner if he *doesn't feel safe*. A student who feels safe is free to confront his daily schedule with enthusiasm, and he can focus concentration on learning. Such a student is more likely to achieve and excel scholastically, and to embrace the challenge of making and sustaining friendships.

A child can't be a learner if he doesn't feel safe.

Students Go to Work Each Day

Children, like adults, go to work each day. School is their workplace. The adult work environment and the child's schoolplace are surprisingly similar. Students must confront people, paperwork, and pressures. Learning is tough stuff. The atmosphere is often one of frustration, competition, and challenge.

Each student, provided he doesn't get fired (expelled), laid off (removed from the classroom), or quit (drop out), spends a great deal of time in the school environment over the course of a 13-year "career." Like me on my American Airlines flight to New York City, the student must feel safe. Unfortunately, the school place isn't always the carefree environment we might like to believe it is. Students have fears ranging from the fear of walking alone through the back corridors to anxiety over what other students think about them.

Surprising as it sounds, many students are fearful while they are at school or at school-related functions. Students are most distressed when they fear another student, when school activities are not well-supervised, when they hear about an incident of violence, or when they are themselves the victims of violence. Young children often fear the unknown disciplinary techniques that a teacher may use "if they are not good." Timid or shy older children may fear a teacher or classmates. These fears have repercussions. Stuttering, bed-wetting, nail-biting, thumb-sucking, nightmares, headaches, and stomachaches are all stress responses — physical manifestations of fear.

In my 20 some years of conducting inservices in the nation's schools, I find many teachers consider their school safer for students than the students themselves do. Yet, a student need not be engaged in a fist-fighting combat with another student to become fearful. Consider the following true incidences.

Physical Safety Is a Prerequisite of Self-Esteem

Trinh, a slender, self-effacing, quiet seventh-grade boy, would make up transparent excuses about headaches, backaches, toothaches — anything to get out of English class. Since he had always liked this class and was a good student, his parents became concerned. After a long talk, his parents found the problem was not academics and grades, as they had thought, but physical security. Trinh was being bullied.

One day two large eighth-grade boys came up to Trinh, pushed him into a locker, shoved him around, and demanded his lunch money. They threatened to beat him up unless he gave them all his money, and a dollar every day from then on. They told him to meet them outside of his English class to give them the money. Trinh handed over his money the first time and tried to ignore them the next day. Again the bullies slammed him around and threatened him. Trinh began giving them money every day. He was afraid to tell anyone because the bullies said if anyone found out they would "get him." Trinh didn't know these boys were doing the same thing to several other students in his class. Everyone was too afraid to talk and the bullies prospered.

Nor are girls free from fears for their physical safety. Darlene, a popular cheerleader, demanded that Karen, a bright but timid classmate, do her Science homework for her each night. When Karen protested, Darlene said that not only would she spread bad rumors about Karen, she would hurt Karen physically. Karen was terrified. When she told her best friend, Leann, what Darlene was doing, Leann confronted Darlene. One day Darlene "accidentally" slipped and knocked Leann down. Because Darlene was popular, no one believed Leann when she said that Darlene had done it on purpose. Leann earned a reputation as a liar and someone jealous of Darlene's popularity; Karen kept on doing the Science homework.

These things can happen to very small children, too. Fourth-grader Sam innocently walked into the school restroom one afternoon, interrupting two sixth-grade boys who were smoking. Shoving Sam up against the wall, they threatened to burn him with the cigarette. When he began to cry, they made fun of him and shoved him harder. Although Sam promised not to tell anyone, the older boys made a point of glaring at him whenever they saw him at recess or in the cafeteria. Sam was terrified and had trouble concentrating for weeks.

An unsafe school environment damages students. Students who are attacked without provocation or students who do not know their assailants experience prolonged levels of anxiety, stress, and depression. The victim of a physical assault isn't the only one hurt. All students are indirectly affected by the threat of physical

A student need not be engaged in fist fights to become fearful.

or emotional harm in the schoolplace. When a child views school as a hostile environment, he is more likely to dislike school, teachers, and fellow students. Research shows that youth who are afraid at school are more likely to rate themselves as below-average students. Fearful students actually do receive lower grades.

Fear reduces a student's ability to concentrate on schoolwork and creates an atmosphere of mistrust. It undermines morale and conveys the impression that the staff is not in control. Students sense that disorder is more powerful than the adult call for order.

All students are affected by the threat of physical or emotional harm in the schoolplace.

Student-victims of attack, robbery, or verbal abuse often admit they are afraid as they go on the way to and from school, and while they are actually in school. If their uneasiness becomes intolerable, they stay away from school altogether. Currently, more than one million children drop out of school each year, and the figure continues to increase. To what extent is personal safety a factor?

Many students are unable to strike back when they become the target of violence or hostility. These children are more susceptible to stress-related illness because they have an impaired ability to deal effectively with fear or anger. Instead, they internalize their fear or rage. Because children don't receive training to prepare them for the threat of violence in school, many are ill-equipped to confront the dangers they find there.

Do Your Students Feel Safe at School?

No one expects you to bolster sagging ceilings to make students more secure as they walk under them, or to install brighter lights to illuminate mysterious and intimidating corridors, or to frisk everyone for anything that might be construed as a weapon. You are an educator, not a security expert. Yet, your students do look to you for protection. As an educator, one of your responsibilities is to help students feel they are in an environment where they can concentrate on learning, rather than on surviving real or imaginary dangers. What *can* you do?

■ **Be aware.** Be aware of your students' fears and anxieties about their physical safety. The areas in the schoolplace that account for some of the big fears include:

The restrooms: Students fear encountering other students there who will "rough them up" in order to make them keep secrets from the school staff or other students about using drugs or smoking.

The bus: Students fear rowdy, aggressive, and verbally abusive students who force them to leave a favored seat, or who rough them up "just for the fun of it."

The empty hallway: Students fear encountering the school tough guys while they are walking alone.

The lunch room: Students fear being shoved, poked, or being pushed out of their place in line, or having their food taken by another student.

The unsupervised classroom or hallway: Students fear getting into a fight with another student and being hurt or embarrassed in front of other students.

The principal's office: All students, even the tough guys, fear going to the office when discipline is the issue.

People can frighten students, too. Students may be afraid of the people they encounter during the school day:

Bullies: Every school has tough guys, or tough girls, who seem to enjoy picking on those who show fear.

Foreign students: Some students are afraid to be around people they can't understand, or those who speak another language. Some students believe that foreign students are talking about and making fun of them.

Teachers: Some teachers project a very stern image, making them scary just to look at or think about. Once students get to know them, the fear is dispelled.

■ **Don't underestimate or ignore students' fears.** The expectation of a stressful event can be every bit as potent as the event itself. Adolescents, like young children, need to feel that they can turn to trusted adults for help when it's needed. This reduces feelings of helplessness. Teach students what to do, what to say, how to conduct themselves, and where to turn for help should they encounter fearful situations.

■ **Don't hesitate to intervene.** Talk with your staff about what rules and policies exist to protect students, and make sure that students are familiar with them. Children who want the attention and admiration of older children may become willing victims, often giving up money or possessions in exchange for group friendship. Discuss these issues with your students. Ask parents to be sensitive to their children's stress and struggles. Many fathers tell me that they think their children (especially sons) should "fight it out and solve their own problems because it builds character." That's simply not the case. Leaving a child to fight his battles alone is more likely to lead to feelings of abandonment, fear, depression, mistrust, low grades, and eventually, emotional or physical drop-out.

■ **Teach self-management skills.** Although an incident may not seem serious to you, it's the student's perception that counts. Hear students out, then decide *how* to help. Many young people endure harassment from other students and either cannot resolve it, or are paralyzed by fear. Self-management skills can help prevent this. Assertiveness training, problem-solving, and conflict management are skills worth teaching your students. Confidence adds to your students' sense of personal power and helps them protect themselves. You also may want to refer parents to their local community education programs for workshops and courses. When these skills are missing in children, parents tend to have limited self-management skills as well. There are a number of books on these topics.

The expectation of a stressful event can be as potent as the event itself.

The reference section at the back of this book highlights many sources. You may want to ask your school counselor or librarian to suggest others.

■ **Make students and parents aware of the classroom rules and procedures.** The rules you put in place to govern physical safety in the classroom are to protect *all* students. Posted rules, as well as emergency safety procedures, make it clear to each student that you value the safety of all the children in the room. Be sure that parents know what the rules are, and *why* and *how* they are designed to protect their children. Ask parents to support the rules by encouraging their children to adhere to them.

■ **Make students and parents aware of the policies that govern school-wide safety.** Be sure that parents are aware of the rules that exist for student safety in the school environment. Again, be sure that each child knows what the rules are, and ask parents to encourage their children to follow them.

■ **Learn about school security.** Security procedures are necessary in every school. The best procedures are unobtrusive. If rules are lacking or not enforced in your school, arrange to meet with the principal and your teacher representation board to discuss what can be done. Measures to ensure physical security must focus on guaranteeing internal control of the school and external control of its perimeter. Take the time to talk to the school principal, groundskeeper, or security officer about what safety measures are being used on your school campus. Do teachers regularly walk through corridors and grounds? Is the cafeteria supervised? Are all school-related functions well supervised? Is the student-teacher ratio manageable? Does a patrol car come by to check out the parking lot during evening activities? Is the campus well lighted at night?

■ **Listen to the stories your students share about other teachers.** Do students sound truly frightened, upset, or insecure? Do they seem embarrassed when talking about something a particular teacher said or did? Do they sound as if they are holding back anything? Ask about how other students in the class view the teacher or school personnel. Though we don't like to admit it, sexual overtures can and do happen in the schoolplace. Sexual abuse or mental cruelty have a devastating effect, even on students who are not directly involved.

School Is Only Part of the Student's Day

While our primary area of concern is the classroom, we also should be concerned with how students fare at home. Children who come from frightening neighborhoods or unsafe homes spend their day in emotional turmoil. Quite naturally, their minds are not on their studies. Doing your best to make your students feel safe and secure means understanding where they are coming from . . . literally.

The more parents learn about their children's feelings of safety, real or imagined, the more they can make the home a safe haven. Would you shop at a mall if

Confidence adds to your students' sense of personal power.

you were afraid to walk alone to your car? Would you stay in your teaching position if you were afraid to walk from your car to the school, or if you were afraid to walk to your classroom alone before, after, or during school? Would you stay if you were afraid of your students or other teachers? Would you break up a fight between two students if you felt they would hurt you in the process? Probably not. Today, many children feel fearful, and what's more, many feel alone with their fears.

Many children feel alone in their fears.

Safety Begins at Home

Ask parents to take the time to view safety from the child's perspective. The following questions can help parents determine whether their home environment is one in which their child *is* safe, and *feels* physically safe. Ask parents to ask their children these questions, and listen closely to each child's response — not just the response the parent expects to hear.

- Does my child *feel* we live in a *safe* neighborhood? Why? Why not?
- Are there neighbors my child feels comfortable asking for help should he need it if I'm not around?
- How safe is my home?
- Are there places in our home that are frightening to him?
- How much time does he spend alone at home?
- Does she know what to do, whom to call, where to go in case of an emergency, if I am not there? Have we discussed (for small children) how to use the telephone? Is it where she can reach it?
- Does my child look forward to coming home? Is he eager to spend time at home, or does he try to stay away as much as possible?
- Does she seem comfortable to stay home with siblings, the other parent, or is she disturbed when I'm not around?
- Does my child fear anyone associated with his home, including parents, siblings, or service people?
- Is my child proud to bring friends home? Does she show off her home, especially her room?
- Does my child, especially in the teen years, feel that this is "my home," not just "my parents' home?"
- Does my child fear spending time alone?
- Is my child afraid of *me*?
- What is my philosophy of discipline. Is it fair or harsh?
- Who disciplines my child beside me? What is *their* approach to discipline?
- What *are* my child's fears?

Parents and Children Have Different Perceptions

When parents and children answer these questions, the children's responses often differ from the way parents say their children will respond. Most parents are surprised to learn how children really view their home place. For example, last year more than 63% of children came home to an empty house. These are our "latch-key" children. Most parents said their children were well briefed about staying safe, yet nearly two-thirds of these children said they were afraid to be home alone while their parents were away. Of the children who came home to caretakers other than their parents, 17% expressed a deep fear of the person put in charge to protect them. Most surprising of all, 12% of all children feared one or both of their biological parents, and more than half said they were fearful of a stepparent.

How many of your students do you suspect do not feel safe in their home environment? What posture does your school take regarding physical abuse?

Two-thirds of the children surveyed said they were afraid to be home alone.

Sexual Abuse Is Cruel

Being sexually victimized takes an enormous toll on the value a child places on her self worth. Sexual abuse creates not only trauma for the child, but renders her incapable of building her self-esteem. A child who falls victim to sexual abuse suffers physical hurt and psychic pain that can last a lifetime. It also can result in her hurting others. Research shows that sexually abused victims often repeat the cycle with their children.

If you suspect that a student is being sexually abused, report it. Most schools not only require by law that you do so, but support the school's responsibility by investigating cases. Ask your school counselor to provide parents with preventative and intervention materials, as well as literature and information hotlines. Many communities have crisis centers to help parents learn how to overcome these destructive actions toward children. These centers can help a parent who suspects or knows that the parenting partner is molesting a child, even when the suspicious parent may be afraid to do something for fear of retaliation. Many parents need and want to know where to go to seek help — for themselves, and their children. *Educators are advocates for children's safety, as well as instructors.*

Teaching Parents to Effectively Discipline Their Children

All of us are afraid to be hurt by someone who is bigger and more powerful than we are. And that's what physical punishment represents to children. Punishment should teach children there are boundaries for behavior and consequences for not adhering to those boundaries. All schools need to offer workshops to parents on effective ways to guide and discipline their children. All too often, parents discipline a child based on crises, moods, or frustration rather than on the values he or she wants to instill in the child.

Like teaching, parenting requires thought, not just action. More and more parents are turning to schools on help in learning effective parenting skills. A good parenting workshop can help parents understand their children's behavior and see it for what it is. Workshops can teach parents the skills they need to effectively discipline their children and bring about good behavior. In addition, workshops can teach parents how to win their children's cooperation and respect, how to set reasonable expectations, how to teach children to be responsible, and how to determine appropriate consequences for their children's inappropriate actions.

Parents, too, need to think about what they're doing — the why of what they do. They need to understand how their parenting actions influence their child's self-esteem.

Educators are advocates for children's safety, as well as instructors.

Discussion

Student safety *is* your concern. The first and most fundamental aspect of self-esteem is a strong sense of physical safety. Take a moment now to evaluate your school. Here are some very important questions for you to address:

1. What do you do in *your* classroom to allow students to feel safe? For example, perhaps you have established two to four safety rules explaining acceptable behavior, and the consequences if the rules are not obeyed. Such safety rules send a loud and clear message that you will see to it that all students are safe in your room. They can *count* on you to protect them. List the safety rules that are currently displayed and enforced in your room. Are they adequate? Is your list too long? Has your staff agreed on basic rules that are consistently enforced in each classroom?

2. Why are these rules important? Or are they?

3. All students want to know the boundaries of each rule. Know that all rules will be tested. A rule that says, "No hitting, kicking, biting, or throwing others out the window," for example, will be tested: "Does the teacher mean always? What about when she's tired, busy, or in an especially good mood? Does she enforce rules on Friday afternoon in the same manner as on Monday morning?" What stop-gap measures do you use for boundary testing?

4. What safety measures are enforced in the school environment? What else needs to be done?

5. List the safety rules that are currently displayed and enforced on the school grounds. What else needs to be done?

6. What measures are in place to protect the well-being of staff members at your school? Are they satisfactory? Do all teachers feel safe — always?

7. How can you evaluate physical safety in your students' homes? What criteria should you use?

8. How can you identify home situations that may be unsafe? What can you do to help children in unsafe homes?

9. How can you tell whether a child's safety fears are valid or invalid?

Chapter 5

EMOTIONAL SECURITY:
Helping Students Feel Worthy

The second building block of self-esteem is emotional security. When a student feels emotionally secure, she isn't fearful of being "beat up" emotionally or being made to feel unworthy. She isn't afraid she'll be made to feel "less" at the expense of someone else needing to feel "more." She feels safe from intimidation or emotionally painful put-downs.

Think how demeaning it is when someone makes you feel unimportant, says something unkind or sarcastic, or doesn't show respect or pay attention when you're talking. Yet, we often say thoughtless things to students, sometimes even in front of their peers, that we wouldn't say to friends or colleagues. These put-downs "tear down" — they hurt, and the effects last. A child believes what she hears. A child's mind is like a tape recorder, storing all incoming messages. The messages are played back later, and they become her reference for what she believes about herself. This tape makes up her "inner language," and it becomes the voice telling her what she can or can't do. For better or for worse, a child is "programmed." Have you ever persevered through difficult undertakings against all odds because you believed you could? Have you ever sabotaged your own efforts, even though you knew that it would prevent you from achieving what you wanted? Just as positive statements are self-esteem building, negative statements are detrimental to self-esteem.

> **Negative "self-statements" are detrimental to self-esteem.**

Our inner language has a powerful effect on us. Inner language creates our reality. In the first 16 years of life, this tape is largely constructed by parents and educators. Positive or negative, these messages have long-term implications. I've worked with some students who no longer rely on others to put them down — they do it for themselves! Many children carry the scars of hurtful words from their childhood into their adult years.

Put-Downs Tear Down

Several months ago, I attended a four-day event for my 16-year-old daughter in a small town on the northern California coastline. The third evening was planned just for the 100-plus young people in this competition, so parents were on their own. I asked around where I might have an informal dinner at an outdoor cafe, and was told to go to "restaurant row." When I arrived at the parking lot serving this group of specialty shops and restaurants, I was informed that the parking lot was full, so I parked elsewhere — nearly a mile away as it turned out. Taking a shortcut, I drove through that same parking lot to reach the restaurant.

Parked in this lot that was supposedly full was an old, very big Cadillac. The car had been pulled lengthwise — oblivious to the painted white lines — across four parking spaces! Nearing the badly dented and dirty vehicle, I saw a large dog was hanging out the open window. He bared his teeth and snarled at me as I drew closer. I was surprised to see, crouching next to the furious dog, a tiny kitten that did not seem at all afraid of this big, snarling beast. But this incongruous pair was not the most contradictory thing I would find.

Now that I was even with the car, I saw it was packed completely full of clothes, as if someone had stuffed it with armfuls of laundry. From door to door, from the dashboard to the back windows, the clothes were packed solid. The dog and kitten couldn't help but tread on them.

Seated on the driver's side was a large woman. She glanced up from her crocheting and said in a friendly and feminine voice, "Hi, I'm Margaret." She smiled, her eyes sparkling and her words seeming to dance as she spoke. It was hard to tell, but she looked about 35 or 40.

I wanted so badly to ask, "How on earth did you create this mess? What do you do? How long have you been here? How can you stand it with those clothes packed in all around you?" I also considered asking why she was thoughtlessly taking up four parking spaces in such a crowded lot. Instead, I said, "It's a beautiful evening, don't you think? Are you waiting to join friends for dinner?"

"Oh no," she replied. "I don't have any friends. I'll just be here in the car." Although her response was dismaying, she sounded content.

"How long have you been here?" I asked, trying not to stare at the mess.

"A long time," she replied, smiling brightly.

I didn't think she understood me. "What I meant is that it looks as if the clothes were packed in around after you got in the car. It looks like you've been sitting for some time."

"Well, honey, I have been here a pretty long time. I live in my car."

"Really? You live in your car?" That would explain her oily and uncombed hair. "What do you do when you want to shower?" I asked, trying to be as polite as I could.

"I go over there," Margaret said, pointing one of her crochet needles toward the nearby Best Western hotel. "I take the elevator to the second floor and wait for someone to leave their room. Then I ask them if I might use their shower."

"That's certainly innovative," I said, wondering whether hotel guests might grant such a bold request. "Does it always work for you?"

"Well, of course not!" she said, sounding a bit shocked. "You can imagine that some people say no. After all, the guests use credit cards to pay for their stay and some people are afraid I might use their phone and charge credit card calls on their bills. Others are afraid I might stay in the room for the afternoon and cause them to be charged for an extra day. And some folks are afraid I might stay several days. I don't always get a thumbs up, but sometimes I do."

As far as I could tell, Margaret didn't appear to be destitute. Plus, she possessed an articulate vocabulary and some important social skills — she was friendly and outgoing, and perhaps she knew something about credit card billing cycles that I didn't. My curiosity prompted me to press on. "Why do you live in your car?"

At that question, her voice lost its confident tone and she hung her head. "It's like this," she began. "My tenth-grade teacher said I'd never amount to much and I guess she was right. My dad said so, too. 'Margaret,' he would say, 'you'll end up a bum, or you'll marry one.' And I did — I married an alcoholic bum just like my dad. My husband left me a year after we were married. Then my boss fired me — I guess he thought I was a nothing, too. I suppose I'm what they said I am."

"Isn't there anyone in your family you can turn to?" I asked, wanting to break the saga of how everyone had done her in.

Margaret shook her head sadly. "I have a sister who lives across town. She's a cop, but she won't give me any money. She won't even talk to me. I guess I embarrass her."

I realized we were back to square one. "Well, surely there's some place where you can get help. A half-way house perhaps."

"Are you kidding?" Margaret said, waving her crochet needle for emphasis. "This town has those kinds of places for men, but not for women."

It was obvious that she was blaming her gender for her victimization. By now, I was beginning to understand that her story was a long series of negative events, so I tried another tack. Seeing the colorful, crocheted doilies stacked on the dashboard and the afghan knitted of the same colors that was wrapped around her shoulders, I figured she had to make money somehow. I said, "The afghan you're wearing is beautiful. Did you knit it? Do you take your work to stores that sell knitted things on commission?"

"Naww," she drawled, her tone of voice sounding distressed, her vocabulary losing all its poetic grace. She would no longer look at me. "Who would want these worthless things?"

I was about ready to give up, but I tried one more approach. "Isn't there something you want more than anything else? A goal of some kind?"

Her eyes lit up with longing. "Oh, that's easy! I want to be able to take a bath at any time without having to ask. I'd like to have my own place!"

My spirits soared. Now, we were getting somewhere! "Well, if I come here next year, where will I find you? Where will you be?"

"Right here, honey," she said, smiling sweetly. "I'm not going anywhere."

I believed her. I excused myself for dinner.

> "I suppose I am what they said I am."

Who Imprisoned Margaret?

Why couldn't Margaret transform her life? Why couldn't she attain her goal to have a place of her own? How could such a friendly, communicative, intelligent woman not be able to start over? Margaret couldn't start over because she was stopped by her inner language. Her inner tape was a destructive collection of negative statements reminding her that she "couldn't," "wouldn't," "shouldn't" and so, she "didn't." Although Margaret had a high school diploma, a year-and-a-half of college, a job, and once had a marriage partner — all the things that so many strive for — the good life eluded her. Perhaps Margaret sabotaged herself. Acting from the messages that contributed to her low self-esteem, she saw few options to transform her life, and hence, she gave up.

How many students do you know with a defective inner tape? How many, either now or in the future, will end up sitting in someone else's parking spaces? You see, Margaret couldn't be socially responsible because she had not yet become personally responsible! Unable to care for herself, she simply was unable to care about the rights of others. You have to be personally responsible before you can be concerned about the well-being of others.

Children believe what they hear and act on it.

That we *can become what we believe* is the good news — if what we believe builds self-esteem. It's important that what our children hear about themselves builds positive self-esteem. Children believe what they hear, and act on it. I'm reminded of a story I heard Gail Dusa of the National Counsel for Self-Esteem tell at the National Council meeting in Santa Barbara, California. A young boy came home crying because a classmate had called him a sissy.

"Why are you crying?" his grandmother asked.

"Because Paul called me a sissy. Do you think I'm a sissy, Grandma?"

"Oh no," said the grandmother. "I think you're a Ferrari."

"What?" said the boy, trying to make sense of what his grandmother had said. "Why do you think I'm a car?"

"Well, if you believe that because Paul called you a sissy, you are, you might as well believe you're a car. Why be a sissy when you can be a Ferrari!"

"Oh," exclaimed the boy gleefully, feeling quite relieved. "I get to decide what I am!"

And that is, in effect, what we need to help our students believe: **Why be a sissy when you can be a Ferrari!** If enough significant people in our students' lives help them to ground that simple but important concept, our students will, too. We want our young people to believe in the "believe, achieve, succeed" ideology.

"Sticks and stones" aside, words *can* hurt. But words also build students up, instill self-confidence and self-acceptance, and influence how students view themselves and react to their surroundings now, and later in life. Taking the time, effort, and thought required to empower your students' inner language is one of the most important aspects of teaching.

Helping Students Develop a Positive Inner Tape

How can you help a student develop positive inner messages, especially when he gives himself negative messages that only serve to defeat him? Self-statements such as "I can't," "I'm fat," "I'm ugly," or "I'm dumb," do little to promote a positive sense of self-regard. You can help your students develop a healthy inner tape or even reprogram an existing negative one. Here are the steps.

■ **Use positive language.** The first step is to assess the kind of language *you* use. Is it positive and optimistic, supportive and encouraging? What is the nature of *your* language? Do you encourage your students and build their self-esteem? Do they hear that they're worthwhile, capable, and special to you? What do your words and actions tell your students about acceptance? There are hundreds of opportunities to praise students. Even when correcting a student, use positive and constructive feedback. When you need to call a student to task, make your point, get the message across, but don't demean the student in the process. Focus on the behavior or the work that is not meeting appropriate standards. Even if a student is doing poorly, phrase your comments so that she knows you're telling her this because you want to help her, and because you know she can do better — you're not just being critical. In other words, keep the student's self-esteem high while correcting an unwanted action. Critique the task, not the child.

■ **Label the language.** Use terms to depict positive esteem-building language. Call them "fuzzies" or "compliments." Label inappropriate language as a "zinger," or a "put-down." Teach these to your students, and then consistently enforce them in the classroom. For example, if a student makes a put-down statement, say, "That's a zinger," or, "That's a put-down." Identifying these polarities provides a reference point so that the student knows the difference between a positive statement and a put-down.

■ **Insist on positive language.** Insist on positive language from everyone in your classroom. Again, the most obvious place to start is with *your* language. Don't talk negatively about yourself or others, and request the same from all students. Post a visual reminder on a bulletin board or door. Some teachers use a card that reads, "Harsh words are hurtful. You don't have the right to hurt anyone in this classroom." When anyone delivers zingers — the put-downs that tear down — the card shows up on his desk as a reminder of just how powerfully words can hurt. Often students are not aware of how many negative self-statements they make, especially to fellow students.

■ **Reinforce positive statements.** Teach students what constitutes a positive statement. Many children have used put-down statements so often they've actually conditioned themselves to believe negative things. If you believe a student is developing negative self-talk, reinforce what you want her to tell herself. If she is really negative, focus on her positive statements and forget the negative ones for awhile. It's easier to change behavior by focusing on the positive aspects instead of the negative.

Keep the student's self-esteem high while correcting unwanted action.

■ **One put-down equals one put-up.** Whenever a put-down is stated, ask the sender to change the put-down into a "put-up." For example, if a student says, "My history teacher is so stupid," say, "That's a zinger." Then, ask him for a "put-up." He may say, "I like my teacher, but I don't think I like to do all the work that is required in History class!" Consistently enforce this rule to divert negative statements and encourage positive language.

■ **Teach students how to receive and give compliments.** Encourage students to praise and compliment others. These statements represent examples of common courtesy: "I appreciate it when you . . ." "I feel good about myself when I . . ." "I really like it when you . . ." "Thanks for noticing." "When you help me I feel . . ." All students from the first grade up should use them.

As you know, not all students have a positive inner language. Sometimes a child needs to replace his inner tape with a new one. It can be done. And, you can withstand the negative reactions from the low self-esteem student without letting your own self-esteem take a beating.

Working with the Low Self-Esteem Student

Students are not aware of how many negative self-statements they make.

There's something you should know about working with a hard-to-like, tough-to-work-with, and sometimes, ungrateful low self-esteem student. Just as your self-esteem cannot be healthy one day and then be completely diminished by the events that happen the next, neither can you turn a poor image into a positive one overnight. It will take dedicated educators and a support staff nearly the school year to turn the poor self-image of a student into a positive one. Here's why.

Let's say you've been told by many exemplary educators that you're not a good classroom teacher. You soon believe that you must be a terrible teacher. Then one day I stop by your classroom for a few minutes and tell you that you are a brilliant teacher. Would you believe me? Probably not. My comment will be met with disbelief. Likewise, if a child has received years of feedback telling him that he's a behavior problem and a good-for-nothing, and it can be confirmed just by adding up the number of times he's been removed from classes or failed courses, then his feelings of self-worth are bound to be low.

Meet Bill

Bill is a student with a bad attitude, poor grades, and a real tough-looking group of friends. He's had years of practice at failing, except at being a tough guy — his friends confirm that he succeeds in that area. Now you want to change his expectations for himself. You tell him he has potential and can do it if he'll just apply himself, and that he doesn't have to be the school bully. Naturally, your projection of his new-and-improved self will be met with disbelief, too. Not only is it unbelievable to him, but it is funny as well. He's serious when he calls you "crazy." But that doesn't mean that his low self-esteem *can't* be transformed into a positive one. It can be done. As I mentioned earlier, there are a number of practices that give us our self-image. These are not put in place overnight.

So, you look over your new group of students and there sits Bill. You intuitively know there are tough times ahead. What do you do? Will you choose to be Teacher A, B, or C?

Teacher A observes Bill over the course of the first few weeks of class, taking note of his low self-esteem as a possible cause for his uncooperative behavior. She sees potential in Bill, and commits herself to helping him see it, too. She sets out a plan of action that includes staying positive even when he is not; she "gets in his face" as students call it, setting goals and expectations for Bill, then gently but diligently insisting that he adhere to them. His aloof and obstinate behavior does not rock her resolve to hold him accountable.

Teacher B observes this low self-esteem child, decides she will work with him to improve his self-esteem, but when he begins to show signs of being uninterested in her help and rejects her efforts, she decides Bill isn't worth the time and attention. After all, there are so many other students, and so little time.

Teacher C observes Bill, and at the outset decides she will not spend her time on a student who is so unwilling to focus on his role as a student. She checks with the counseling office to see if she can get him referred to a special classroom, or placed with another teacher "who works well with kids like Bill." If that doesn't work, she will let him stay in class as long as he is quiet and doesn't disturb the other students, or her.

Needless to say, Bill's only chance of emerging with an improved self-esteem is with Teacher A. Why? Because under her care and rigor, Bill won't have the chance to inflict his low self-esteem behaviors on himself or others for very long. She will work with him and encourage him to confront those areas that reinforce his low self-esteem and help him produce positive inner tapes for himself. Rather than seeing himself as a loser, Teacher A will demand that Bill view himself through a different, more positive lens. She will enlist his support in accomplishing this. Teacher A will be his lifeline to creating a new paradigm, and a new reality.

It won't be an easy nine months for this teacher. In fact, it will be downright difficult. That's because as Bill decides to rethink his image, he'll test the boundaries to see if the teacher really means it. The more fair and dedicated she is to her cause, the more he resists. He thinks, "Surely, she will give up on me like Mom or Dad or Teacher B, C, D, and F did! Surely, she isn't serious! How could anyone believe in me? After all, I don't!" But one day he, too, will believe he is capable and worthy.

One thing is for sure, *he will never forget this teacher*. And the lesson he has learned from her will be an unforgettable one of tenacity, courage, responsibility, respect, caring, and honor. In his lifetime, he will aspire to and achieve whatever he decides to do. He will lecture his children and employees based on what he learned when this teacher worked with him. He will dedicate speeches to her as he picks up tokens and honors of recognition that others have bestowed on him — and there will be many. Bill will make his life a success.

> **Sometimes the projection of a new-and-improved self will be met with disbelief.**

Self-Esteem Is the Key to "At Risk" Intervention

In a study spanning 20 years, psychologist Emmy Werner attempted to identify some of the individual, family, and cultural factors that increase or decrease a child's risk of developing serious problems in life. Werner and a team of physicians, nurses, social workers, and psychologists followed the development of nearly 1,000 children of divorced or troubled parents through young adulthood. Nearly one-third of the children in the study experienced a difficult and turbulent childhood. Of those, one in five developed serious problems by age 17. By late adolescence, 15% had a record of serious or repeated delinquency. Most of the children in the study, however, did not get into trouble. The researchers were impressed by the resiliency of the overwhelming majority of these children. Even among the high-risk children — those who had records, and those who showed at least four risk factors by age 10 — one-fourth developed into stable, mature, and competent young adults. Moreover, they expressed a high degree of faith in the effectiveness of their own actions.

Students will always test the boundaries to see if you are serious.

How did these resilient children differ from their more troubled peers? The most striking characteristic that emerged was that these children had been underdogs, but were fortunate enough to have had someone who cared enough to get involved. What's even more interesting is that these very children were then able to lend emotional and physical support to someone else in need. They became care-givers who assumed responsibility for helping others. The feeling of being needed and the emotional support provided by these care-givers in return, was a major protective factor in the midst of chronic poverty and/or serious family disruptions. These same children expressed a higher degree of satisfaction in helping others in later life, too.

Other studies confirm these results. A long-term Harvard study begun 40 years ago in an effort to understand juvenile delinquency followed the lives of nearly 500 teenage children, many of whom were from impoverished or broken homes. When the subjects were compared at middle age, one fact stood out: regardless of intelligence, family income, ethnic background, or amount of education, those who had responsibilities in shared home- and work-projects as children, even if this meant only simple household chores, enjoyed happier and more productive lives than those who had not had such responsibilities. When these individuals reached adulthood, they were better off than their childhood playmates who had been less industrious. They earned more money, and had more job satisfaction. They had better marriages and closer relationships with their children. They had productive and satisfying relationships with co-workers. They were healthier and lived longer. Above all, they were far happier.

Discussion

1. What do you do to build emotional security for students in your classroom? What else needs to be done?

2. How is emotional security provided for in the school environment? What else needs to be done?

3. How do your colleagues enhance and promote a climate of emotional security? What else needs to be done?

Exercise

1. Have a round-table class discussion about name-calling and how it feels, and what students can say in return to discourage the other student. Role playing is an effective way to conduct this kind of teaching.

2. Have students write positive, neutral, and negative ways to make a point. Examples:

Negative: Geez, when was the last time you brushed your teeth, Christmas?

Positive: My mom gave me a package of Lifesaver Breath Mints; I'm eating one, would you like one?

Negative: You never shut up and have to comment on everything all the time.

Positive: I like how open you are and willing to communicate. People learn a lot from listening to you, but maybe you could listen to other people sometimes and learn from them, too.

3. Have students write essays on a time when their feelings were hurt by parental name-calling. Without putting names on the papers, share them with parents and help parents understand the benefit of positive language and its contribution to their child's self-esteem.

Chapter 6

EMOTIONAL SECURITY:
Dealing with Students' Fears and Insecurities

The second facet of a child's sense of emotional security largely has to do with coping with his own psychology. Here, the educator's job is to assist him in understanding and dealing with intrinsic fears and insecurities, and to help him feel capable of transcending them.

The more we know about the psychology of each age in the childhood years — what it's like being age 2 or 5, 6 or 9, 11 or 17 — the more we learn about the nature of childhood. What we have discovered is that children are more vulnerable to specific anxieties at certain ages than at others. For example, at age 14, a child's primary need is for *unconditional acceptance* of himself as an individual. He wants to be accepted, no matter what. Long hair, green hair, or shaved hair, his actions center on gaining approval and total acceptance for his individual sense of self. And he uses whatever strategy works! This necessary and natural developmental stage is called *seeking autonomy*.

This differs from a 5-year-old, whose primary need is to be *with* his parents, preferably, all the time, and to know about their safety when he is away from them. He'd like to spend all day with them, and even would like to sleep in their room at night! Being without his parents, his greatest fear, causes him great distress. This necessary and natural developmental stage is called *separation anxiety*. Whereas the 14-year-old seeks separation from his parents, the 5-year-old is debilitated by it.

A student's particular stage of development is a factor behind his motivations as reflected by his behavior. By being aware of these developmental stages, you can better understand the work that a child must undertake at each stage and consequently, better understand his behavior. This better enables you to help the student learn acceptable ways to respond to the challenge of learning, to his fellow students and teachers, and adjust to the school environment.

A student's stage of development is a factor behind his motivations.

A Crash Course in Childhood Development

What is the work of childhood? Each stage of a child's development presents its own set of tasks and demands, all focused on gaining self-knowledge — **selfhood**.

The work of each stage is well defined. Though it's not possible to examine each age in detail, I'll give you a general overview to help you decipher how each stage influences a child's perception of self. The suggested reading section at the back of this book provides additional resources, and you may wish to consult your district's child development specialist, psychologist, school nurse, or counselor for additional references.

Psychological Stages and Their Relation to the Development of Self-Esteem

Age 2: Autonomy

Up until the age of 2, a child primarily views himself as part of his mother (or father if he is the primary caretaker). At 2 years, he develops the *ability* to be aware that he is, in reality, separate from his parent. This presents him with the task of establishing autonomy — separateness. The two words that best describe his newfound self-hood are "*No!*" and "*Mine!*" Possession is a tool he uses to enforce his growing sense of separate self.

The 2-year-old is looking for power and ways to assert it.

Implications for Developing Self-Esteem: Parents who have experienced their child's zealous work on this task of self-ness without understanding it call this stage "The Terrible Twos." But the 2-year-old is neither a selfish nor an obstinate child. He's looking for power and ways to assert it. Assisting this child's developing sense of self is a matter of empowering him by providing him ways to be assertive. The parent (or daycare provider) needs to give this child choices. For example, let him pick out which shoes he wants to wear, or how he wants to comb his hair. Let him decide which book you will read to him. In each instance, provide him with two or three choices — all choices that you can live with. The autonomy the young child develops at this stage lays the foundation for being able to value himself. Through his "work" he learns that he can assert himself, the forerunner of independence. If these tasks have been met with a fair degree of success, by age 3, he will be quite independent.

Age 3: Mastery

Having realized his separateness, the 3-year-old goes on to master his environment. Mastery plays an important role in his perception of self: it influences his feeling of being capable (or not being capable). His need for success in his endeavors at this stage is crucial. He labors over each of his accomplishments. He is slow and methodical, and it takes forever to do each task! Needing feedback to know if he has been successful, he strives for recognition of each achievement. He constantly says, "Watch me! Watch me!" That he has something to offer nurtures his sense of competence and proves *to himself* that he is worthwhile.

The search for mastery stimulates a child's curiosity. She wants to know

"Why, why, why?" Her *drive* for discovering and learning is insatiable. In fact, her *capacity* for learning is unlimited. She has an incredible ability to learn languages and language-related skills. She vigorously explores her surroundings, observes people, and examines how she fits into each relationship. Needing to know about everything is a huge assignment for such a little person. This is also a time of sexual unfolding. Here the opposite-sex parent plays a major role in the child's developing sense of self.

Implications for Developing Self-Esteem: Be patient as you answer this child's repeated questions. She is exploring her environment. Recognize her achievements with much praise and tangible signs such as putting her drawings on display. When you talk with her, repeat things she says. Show her you are listening to her. Ask her to tell you again about something she enjoys discussing, such as why she has drawn a certain picture, or why she chose certain colors.

Age 4: Initiative

The 4-year-old's task is developing *self-initiative*, the forerunner of responsibility. This may involve something as simple as taking responsibility for putting his toys away after he's done playing with them. It may be as detailed as making his own bed — complete with crooked sheets, lumpy covers and corners — or as complex as learning to tie his shoelaces. What's most important to him is his having taken it upon himself to do it — he has decided to attempt the task. Taking initiative is the forerunner of *motivation*.

Self-initiative is the forerunner of responsiblity.

Implications for Developing Self-Esteem: This child's attempts should be commended and allowed, whenever possible, to be left exactly as completed by him. Focus your praise not on the *way* the task was done, but on the fact that it was attempted and/or completed. If you want him to improve the way he does something, show him as opposed to telling him. Experience, not words, is his best teacher. This encourages further displays of his initiative, plus it builds self-confidence.

Age 5: Separation Anxiety

Parents are the name of the game for the 5-year-old. At this age, the mother is the center of the child's world. He not only wants to please her, he wants to be near her, talk with her, play with her, go to work with her, help her around the house, or go along on errands. He would prefer to be with her rather than with playmates. This does not mean that the father is left out of the picture. While mother is preferred, father is important, too.

The 5-year-old's adoration of his parents is unquestionably heartwarming. The result is almost totally parent-pleasing behavior. The good news for the educator is that since children transfer their feelings of their parents onto the teacher, teachers at this stage also are adored and loved. The child's basic framework is "I want to be good all the time. I don't want to do any bad things; I'll do whatever you say." Not only does he want to be good (and he means to be good) but he, more often than not, succeeds in being good. In his determination to do everything just right, he'll ask permission for even the simplest thing, even when he needn't, and will then beam with pleasure when you smile and give permission. Later on in this chapter, I'll be using this age to illustrate a point and you'll see how contemporary times create havoc based on this child's developmental needs.

Implications for Developing Self-Esteem: Most important in this period is helping the young student recognize that he is a person in his own right; that "separate" feelings are all right. It is important to allow the student to feel that he is being good, is doing right, and is winning your approval. Because separation anxiety is very real to him, reassure him about his parent's safety. Let him know you and *his parents* are safe, and so is he.

Age 6: Me-ness

"Self-centeredness" comes before "other-centeredness." At the preschool stage, the child discovered he was separate from his parents, but he still kept his parents as the center of his existence. At age 6, he must shift his focus from his parents to himself. Instead of parents or others, he now places himself at the center of his world. Although he appears self-centered, this is an important milestone in his development. He is now ready to undertake the task of discovering his own interests and attempting to understand them.

> "Self-centeredness" comes before "other-centeredness."

Implications for Developing Self-Esteem: Allow the 6-year-old student reasonable room to make some of his own decisions. This doesn't mean you let him have everything he wants; it means that you show acceptance, while simultaneously setting boundaries and limits. Present him with several options for doing things — again, choose options you can live with. Be tolerant with his boasting. Avoid comparing him to his peers — whether in schoolwork or in play-time activities. Strive to build his individual sense of self by designing projects that invite a variety of learning encounters. When you see a particular area that interests him, allow him to delve into it.

Ages 7 to 8: Sameness

Having established a "me," the student moves on. Now the need to be separate takes a back seat to her need to feel "oneness" with her same-age, same-sex peers. As she makes the move from self to others, playmates are the new "reflectors," and friends become more important. Mastery of social and physical skills becomes the common language to gauge how well she's doing.

Implications for Developing Self-Esteem: Students should be encouraged to join same-age groups, and they should be provided with opportunities to develop skills in a variety of activities. Now is the time to learn healthy and positive ways to relate to others — namely, how to acquire and maintain friendships. Teach and reinforce the skills of fairness and cooperation.

Ages 9 to 10: Who Are *People*?

Duality of needs exist for this child — he needs approval, direction, and affirmation of *both* adults and peers. At this stage, the need to be with members of the same sex is a matter of sexual identity. Although outwardly this child may claim and exhibit contempt for the opposite sex, very often she has a secret boyfriend, he a secret girlfriend. Games of boys chasing girls or vice-versa are common. This is a normal part of forming sexual identity. His task here is to learn the ways of being masculine; her task is to learn how to be feminine. Both boys and girls try to learn how males and females behave by imitating the same-sex parent. This plays a part in the development of self. The task of discovering maleness or femaleness is a child's first healthy, safe attempt at romance, and it lays the foundation for future relationships.

Implications for Developing Self-Esteem: Learning about people is the focus at this stage. This is a good age to teach students to perform courtesies such as holding out a coat for someone or opening a door. It's at this stage that boys, in particular, need to learn the difference between being strong and masculine and being rough. Educators must emphasize the importance of not hurting anyone. If a child is rough with pets or other small animals, this may be a show of dominance or strength, and it should be discouraged. Girls need to learn the difference between being feminine and being weak. Educators can help by choosing stories and books that show healthy relationships between boys and girls and what it means to be a mutual friend. This is the age to introduce principles that teach students a sense of caring for others. It's a good time for children to study cultures other than their own, and generally to build social consciousness.

> **This is the age to introduce principles that teach a sense of caring for others.**

Ages 11 to 12: Re-grouping and Taking Stock

This is a comparatively mellow stage that occurs between two major periods of intense growth. It's a time for refining physical and academic competence, as well as deciding what's important and meaningful and what isn't. Students want and need to try on many roles to see which ones feel right. At times, students appear rambunctious, while at other times, they seem to be bystanders of events, but actually they are *observing everything*.

Implications for Developing Self-Esteem: Here modeling plays an important role. Teachers, parents, and coaches should be terrific people who are worth emulating. This is an open-window stage — both boys and girls have a similar capacity for learning and growing. It's a time of relative ease in learning in just about all areas of the curriculum, whether it's gaining skills in music or soccer. Most students have a natural curiosity and an almost uncanny ability to achieve in several areas simultaneously. Be sure to provide this age student with a variety of opportunities for learning and excelling, regardless of IQ or ability grouping.

Ages 13 to 15: Go for It!

All systems are on *go*! A child's need to be physically active, and his curiosity and ability to expand his understanding of the intellectual, social, and spiritual realms are remarkable. Everything is possible, and everything is explored and examined. It's a time of enormous growth in every way. Yet another stage is being left behind. The child stands on the threshold of adolescence. Considering the scope of tasks that must be undertaken at this stage, it's no wonder that it's also a time of chaos. Building a solid sense of self and personal worth is probably the toughest and most important task the child has ever faced. These are uncharted waters and all learning is a process of trial and error. One of the most difficult challenges is coping with physical growing pains. Physical maturation, both internal and external, occurs at an amazing rate. Key hormones are at work, doing their job of moving the child from pre-adolescence to full-scale puberty. The awkwardness of physical growth is coupled with the psychic pain of feeling lonely and alone. The fact that boys are two years behind girls in physical development doesn't help. The two-year time span in development will even leave some girls out of sync with other girls, causing each to question just why she is (or isn't) growing in this way or that way. Boys are often confused (not to mention embarrassed) by voices that sound normal one day only to squeak, crack, or rasp like sandpaper the next.

Considering the scope of tasks that must be undertaken, it's no wonder it's a time of chaos.

Implications for Developing Self-Esteem: We can best help the 13- to 15-year-old maintain high self-esteem by not making him feel guilty when his efforts don't work out. We need to reassure him that his "new" self is a natural stage of growth and development. Help him understand the changes he is undergoing by discussing them with him. Also discuss the pressures he faces, and help him learn how to deal with them. The more we give the adolescent a sense of security, the better he will withstand the outside pressures from becoming what he thinks peers want him to be. Instead, he can develop along the lines of his interests and talents.

Age 16: Excuse Me, but You're in My Way!

This age stands alone because there really is no other age like it. The 16-year-old student often experiences feelings that range from invincible bravado to confusion, embarrassment, guilt, awkwardness, inferiority, ugliness, and fear all in the same day. In fact, the teenager can swing from childish and petulant behaviors to being sedate, or acting rational or irrational, from intellectual to giddy all within the same class hour. Such mood swings occur as the student tries to figure out just who she is and what's going on with her. Often these mood swings shift from easy tears and genuine sobs to in-depth sensitivity, from great insights and sudden bursts of learning to flare-ups of anger or boisterous giggles. It's a time of confusion and uncertainty. Raging hormones are responsible for ups and downs, as well as for sexual feelings changing from ambivalent to specific. The student longs to experience intimacy and her self-esteem is enhanced when she *belongs*. The task is to learn about oneself as a sexual being (hers, femininity; his, masculinity), and how this sexuality is perceived by others.

This is a time of duality. She wants to be with *others,* yet she wants to be *alone*; she *needs* her friends but will sabotage them if they appear to outdo her. She'll cheer for a friend out loud, but secretly wish for her demise. It's a time when she wants total independence but is by no means capable of it. She doesn't really want to live away from her parents, although she believes her parents are stifling her life.

This physical and emotional jumble is hindered by the inability to look ahead and visualize the long-term effects of present behaviors. To tell the student who is skipping class that she might not be admitted to college or to warn the student who is not studying that she is cheating herself out of an education, is virtually meaningless. *Today*, this very moment, is what matters. Feelings of invulnerability and immortality lead youth to behave in reckless ways. The "it-can't-happen-to-me" attitude prevails, as in driving too fast. This is truly a time of identity crisis. Age 16 is an age of frustration.

Implications for Developing Self-Esteem: Seek to understand the 16-year-old as a budding adult rather than a child. Expect defiance. Consider resistance to adult authority, especially authority wielded by parents and teachers, as part of her need for self-ness. This is part of growing independence. She *must* see adults as hopelessly old-fashioned and naive — this helps her complete the act of pulling away and asserting her independence. She is experimenting with the idea that she can manage life on her own. Most pronounced is the tearing away from the same-sex parent, especially if the bond has been a loving and close one. To emotionally leave this loving parent, the child must make the parent wrong — for how could she possibly want to leave someone who is wonderful? It can be a trying time for the educator as well — remember, children transfer bonding with parents onto the teacher.

Consider resistance to adult authority as a part of the need for self-ness.

A great many 16-year-old children actually do leave home (or threaten to) for three or more days during their sixteenth year. (Ever wonder about that student who mysteriously disappeared for a few days, and then showed up back in your class without explanation?) The degree of defiance this child shows her parents and teachers depends upon how parental power has been handled in early childhood. Many 16-year-olds leave home out of frustration and as a way to coerce parents into providing them with a bigger share of self-power in making decisions.

Help the student learn effective ways to communicate, negotiate, and manage frustration. If you teach this age of student, that's good advice for you, too. And don't forget to take your vitamins!

Ages 17 to 18: Establishing Independence

The final stage of development in childhood is establishing total control as an individual person who can assert his or her own independence. In looking beyond being dependent on others to achieving self-dependence, the student must confront three big tasks:

Determining a vocation. "What am I going to do for work during my life and can I afford myself?" is the question that the student must address. Answering this gives his life meaning. Underlying this task is the self-esteem need to be somebody — to experience positive feelings of strength, power, and competence.

Establishing values. The student's goal is to sort out his *own* values and decide which ones to keep and which ones to discard. This is the only way he can develop integrity with himself. Perhaps most striking is his need to establish a workable and meaningful philosophy of life — to search for his own personal beliefs, and face religious, ethical, and value-laden ideologies. Developing personal convictions will be influenced by his level of self-esteem — especially if there are conflicts between what he believes, what he was raised with, and what his friends find acceptable. Will he stay committed to what is true for him? As he ponders the thought, he'll grasp and cling to a variety of ideals, searching for what they mean as he tries them on for size.

Establishing self-reliance. Accomplishing this task encourages self-trust and confidence. Underlying this is the self-esteem need to be oneself. The student needs to be defined by his own lens, and not by his role as student, athlete, or son.

Implications for Developing Self-Esteem: Show respect for this child as an *individual.* Don't expect him to be a clone, or to parrot your values or the values of other students. In discussions or disagreements, give him the respect you give an adult friend. Ask him for his opinions on adult topics. Ask him to write about his opinions on moral issues, job decisions, or personal problems. Encourage him to think through his own philosophy, and give it more form and substance by putting it into words. He'll need to see that you respect him, that you are helping him learn the process of decision-making, evaluating the consequences, and learning how to put one foot in front of the other in order to go forward with *his* life.

In discussions, give him the respect you give an adult friend.

Do You Know Enough About Your Students?

Educators are often well-trained in teaching in our content area, and in managing children's behavior. But do we know enough about what makes the child-as-person tick? It's helpful to think of a student as a person who is always in transition from one developmental stage to the next. In that regard, a child is one who:

1. Is leaving behind the prior stage of development and is moving on to the next developmental stage.

2. When scared or frightened, slips back into the security of the previous stage.

3. Is undergoing a rapid and intense period of physiological and psychological changes.

4. Wants to be independent but doesn't have a backlog of personal experiences to use in functioning independently.

5. Needs to express his needs and to have these needs taken seriously.

6. Has not yet formed a cohesive value system that will support him in what to "live for," so this tremendously important anchor of security is not yet within his grasp.

7. Is locked into financial and emotional dependence on his family.

8. Notices when there are discrepancies between the rules and values claimed by adults and adult behavior.

9. Has the same intense emotional needs and feelings as an adult but generally has limited understanding as to what these emotions mean or how to cope successfully with them in a manner acceptable to adults.

10. Has a strong need for adult guidance as he constructs his own identity and tries to acquire a sense of selfhood that will sustain him.

11. Feels lonely and alone when parents are physically and emotionally absent and needs his parents to:
   - show love and attention,
   - listen and show empathy and patience,
   - offer guidance and direction,
   - allow experiences for positive growth through exploration,
   - encourage separation and independence,
   - help him cope with the crises at hand,
   - model what it's like to be an adult.

12. Is unable to construct a secure self-identity and becomes less competent to meet the inevitable challenges in daily life without adult nurturing.

13. In the absence of adaptive coping skills, becomes debilitated by the ravages of stress.

14. When the family situation is not nurturing or supportive, feels helpless and turns to peers for the fulfillment of his needs.

Every child has the task of growing up — physically, mentally, spiritually, and emotionally. Children need help every step of the way.

Children's New Fears

Knowing about developmental stages is more than just interesting. Used wisely, this information helps us understand children's behavior and develop programs for it, putting into our curriculum the kinds of analogies, stories, and examples that best illustrate the information from the child's reference point and captivate his attention. Let's look at what this means for a 5-year-old student.

Needing his parents is the "stuff" of the 5-year-old. When he's away from the parent, he suffers *separation anxiety*. You and I had separation anxiety when we were 5, and our children's kids will have it, too. But contemporary times have transformed children's normal fears. Today, 5-year-olds worry daily about their parents' *safety* — not just their parents' whereabouts. In other words, the normal fears take on new meaning. The 5-year-old believes if his mother or father goes to work or stays at home during the day that someone will come in the window and harm the parent. He believes if the parent uses an elevator at work, someone will come in and "knife" the parent. He may even believe if the parent goes into a building that is more than two stories high, there's a good chance of that building being destroyed, just like the one he saw blown up on television. Of course, television is his frame of reference for this fear.

Contemporary times have transformed children's normal fears.

The anxiety of being without his parents, then, is transformed into a fear of his parents' harm, or even death. The 5-year-old wonders whether or not a parent will return that day in order to pick him up after school, or come home at the end of a work day. "My mom is picking me up today," "My dad is taking me to the zoo this weekend," he assures you. This daydream, or flashback, occurs three to five times an hour. Here your 5-year-old student is reassuring *himself* that mommy and daddy are "still okay." It's his way of reasoning that his parents *are safe*.

Not All Fears Are Productive

But he's not at his best right now. He's preoccupied, much like you if you're going through a painful separation or divorce, or something else that is emotionally disturbing. Your mind is preoccupied with sorting it out. Children are emotionally distracted, too. Here's what's at stake for all children:

1. The transference of bonding and trust. When a child comes to school, he has to transfer parental bonding and trust to the teacher. When you say, "Sit down, let's . . .," the student needs to comply. He has to form a trusting relationship with you, the teacher, because this relationship becomes a significant link to his learning. We know that students always transfer onto the teacher the same relationship they have with the same-sex parent.

2. Acceptance of others. Students need to show acceptance of other students. When he looks around at other students, he must conclude, "Gosh, there sure are a lot of kids in here. Rather than hit them, I think I'll talk with them!" We call this view of adjusting to others *socialization* in early childhood, *friendship* when children are older, *popularity* when children get to be teens, and *camaraderie* in adulthood. In the workforce we say they are *team players*, have *synergy*, and so on. Acceptance represents respect for others. Children coping with stress and anxiety do not adjust well to other children. They're generally selfish and rude, even hostile. Often they are not liked much by other students. They don't do well in groups, and because they've alienated others, children are unkind to them in return. Dealing with such "communication problems" takes up valuable time that could be used for learning.

3. Learning. Knowing that the major issue for the 5-year-old is parental anxiety, what does that tell us about what needs to be in the curriculum? Certainly, the curriculum needs to feature stories about children — the 5-year-old identifies with them. If stories feature both pets and children, the 5-year-old is even more interested. Adding a plot where a child and an adult interact together, then the 5-year-old is extremely interested. This kind of story meets the young child's emotional security needs. He'll be held a captive and curious learner. When he is drawn into learning things that satisfy his emotional needs, his attention span increases by five to eight minutes. Thus we meet his needs while providing an opportunity for learning to occur. (The reading list that you design for parents should reflect the developmental needs of students.)

When a child is drawn into learning that satisfies emotional needs, his attention span increases.

Why Are Children So Fearful Today?

Why are today's children so fearful? Let's look again at our 5-year old. Why does the 5-year-old conjure up images of a parent being hurt or killed while he is away at school? Increased exposure to violence is one cause. Television, having erased the dividing line between children's and adult programming, exposes children to everything. This can be problematic because the young child who has seen violence on television — or in real life — transposes that image onto what he imagines could happen to his parents.

That's why you *must* ask parents to censure their child's television viewing. I remember, and perhaps you do, too, a time when the adult contradictions and other personal and social realities of adulthood were slowly revealed. Adults didn't swear in the presence of children, and they understood why it was considered harmful. Today we tend to ignore these commonsense practices, probably believing that children will see and hear it all no matter what we do to prevent it. We erroneously believe that it doesn't matter. It does. If we believe that children don't pay a price for being exposed to violent and hostile messages and images, we misunderstand childhood. You see, 5-year-olds can't separate reality from fantasy. If a young child imagines a ghost is in his room, the parent doesn't leave the ghost under the bed, or behind the headboard, right? The parent puts the ghost up in the corner (so to speak) where the child can "see" it. Then, the parent gives it a friendly name and tells the child that it's there to protect him. Since the 5-year-old doesn't have the capacity to make the fear go away, we create a fantasy to help the child deal with his fear. The world of fantasy and imagination helps young children manage their fears.

Making Children's Fears Go Away

How can we dispel fears so that children can be psychologically comfortable enough to go on to other things — things such as being a friend and learner? We need to know and understand what's going on with our students in their specific developmental stage, and then put in place those practices designed to provide emotional security — practices which allow the child to deal with the fear appropriately. Following through on our 5-year-old, here's what you *must* do.

The unknown produces fear for children.

1. Dispel the fear. Ask parents to take their child to visit the parent's workplace. It doesn't have to be Monday morning at 8:00 a.m. It can be in the afternoon at 4:30 p.m., or on a weekend. The goal is to let the child see the parent's workplace *as a safe and orderly environment*, and to give the child reason to believe that the parent is safe there. Many children have never been to their parents' workplace. In fact, most children have no idea of what their parents do during the day. Young children often think that their parents work with dangerous people who carry guns and knives. Even older children are frightened when they believe that their parents' well-being might be in jeopardy. For this reason, ask parents to arrange the visit for a time when several colleagues are at the work place. The *unknown* produces fears for children. This is true for all children, even the 15-year-old who is painfully aware of and often angry about how much he needs adults. These anxieties keep students from the other productive work to be done in childhood, such as making and sustaining friends and, of course, learning.

2. Ask parents to monitor television viewing. Parents *must* monitor television viewing when their children are young. I advise parents to do so until their children are at least 12 years old. Children pay a high price for the violence they see on television. Harmful insecurities are created as a result of the impact of these images on young minds.

3. Talk about parental safety. Ask parents to talk to their children about *their* safety while they are away from their children, especially if the parent travels and is away from home often.

4. Learn about the normal stresses, strains, and fears of childhood. Since many of the fears are predictable at the various ages and stages of development, we should know what they are. This knowledge gives us insight into the motivations of students, shows us where they need extra support and what specific tools they need to manage daily life. In my book, *Stress in Children*, I examined the insecurities at each grade level. Although it's not possible to include all of that research for you here, I'll provide a summary.

Kindergarten:

- Uncertainty of parental safety.
- Fear of abandonment by parents.
- Fear of punishment/reprimand from teachers, parents, or other adults.

First Grade:

- Fear of loud noises, especially that of large trucks and buses.
- Fear of being struck by another student.
- Fear of wetting on themselves in class or in front of others.

Second Grade:

- Fear of not understanding a given lesson (won't be able to spell words for quiz, pass a test).
- Fear of not being asked to be a "teacher's helper."
- Fear of teacher's discipline.

Third Grade:

- Fear of being chosen last on *any* team.
- Fear of not being liked by the teacher.
- Fear of not having enough time to complete work.
- Fear of being asked to stay after school.

Fourth Grade:

- Fear that a friend will betray them, select a different friend, or share "their" secrets.
- Fear of ridicule by teacher or other students.
- Fear of not being personally liked by the teacher.

Fifth Grade:

- Fear of being chosen first on any team (and being made an example).
- Fear of losing his or her best friend or that the friend will share secrets.
- Fear of being unable to complete schoolwork.

Sixth Grade:

- Fear of the unknown concerning his or her own sexuality.
- Fear of not passing into middle school/junior high.
- Fear of peer disapproval of appearance.
- Fear of not being liked by other students.

Seventh Grade:

- Fear of being selected first (and having to lead).
- Fear of being picked last (interpreted as being disliked or unpopular).
- Fear of the unknown concerning his or her own sexuality (peers have shared wild stories or myths, compounded by television exposure and popular song lyrics).
- Extreme concern and worry about emotional happiness and unhappiness.
- Fear of not being able to complete homework/schoolwork/task assignments.

Eighth Grade:

- Fear of being selected last (seen as being disliked or unpopular).
- Fear of coming to terms with own sexuality (based on lack of information concerning his or her sexuality, coupled with fear and anxiety about his or her own "normal" development).
- Extreme concern and worry about emotional happiness and unhappiness.
- Fear of activities that require exposure of the body (P.E. class).

Ninth Grade:

- Fear of sexuality (too much misinformation from peers).
- Fear of activities that require exposure of the body (P.E. class).
- Extreme concern and worry about emotional happiness and unhappiness.
- Fear of being challenged to a confrontation by someone of the same sex (getting into a fight).

Tenth Grade:

- Fear of being disliked or unpopular.
- Fear that another peer will vie for his or her "sweetheart."
- Fear of not having derived satisfaction from schooling ("I'm not a good student"; "I don't do well in school, but I don't know why.").
- Fear of family disharmony.

Eleventh Grade:

- Fear of "not being OK" and being ridiculed by class members.
- Fear of not having enough money.
- Fear that adults will interpret roles for him or her (the student seeks to try on and define his or her own values).
- Concern over not knowing what to do in life.

Twelfth Grade:

- Fear that adults will interpret roles for him or her (wanting to clarify for themselves their values, goals, and relationships).
- Fear of uncertainty (not knowing what to do with his or her life outside of school).
- Fear that preoccupation with self-needs (physical, job, career, personal, peer, ego) have rendered him or her learning deficient ("I didn't take school seriously." "I don't think I learned anything." "I don't think I'll make it in college.").

Talk about these stressors with your students and help them learn effective ways to deal with them. Share them with parents, too. When parents better understand their children's insecurities, and help their children find workable solutions, students will come to the learning experience less emotionally encumbered. Again, there are many excellent books on children's development. Several are listed in the reference section at the back of this book. Ask your school district's curriculum director, or respective director of elementary or secondary education, or your school's counselor or librarian for additional resources. Your knowledge can help you highlight implications for curriculum development, and can assist you in designing parent-education programs.

5. Be alert for the symptoms that show a student is feeling insecure. Physical, emotional, and behavioral symptoms indicate insecurity. Be alert to the student who is withdrawn, sullen, moody, or hostile. Also watch for the student who fights or swears excessively, or the student who suffers psychosomatic illnesses such as persistent stomachaches or headaches. When these symptoms occur for more than seven to 10 days at a time, it's time to determine their causes. When a student is not coping well and you need assistance in helping the student address his problems, turn to your counselor, or the school referral service (if one exists), to schedule a conference to determine intervention strategies.

Physical, emotional, and behavioral symptoms indicate insecurity.

6. Teach stress management skills. Managing stress is critical to each student's ability to move beyond fear and successfully manage the day-to-day events. Being *able* to manage stress helps students to develop confidence in themselves, and in their abilities to handle the stress and strains of childhood and to meet challenges head on. When students feel they are capable and emotionally hearty, their self-esteem is strengthened. Books like *A Stress Management Guide for Young People* provide excellent teaching units for helping students to identify and manage stress. Here are two sample lessons that you can adapt to the level of maturity of your students.

What Causes Stress For You?

Teach students to manage their stress. Can you identify your stressors? The examples shown below are typically stressful for most young people. Read each one and in the spaces provided, add some of your own.

I feel stressed when:

■ My parents are really upset with me.

■ I have an argument with my best friend.

■ I don't have enough money for the things I would like.

■ I feel my appearance is not what I want it to be.

■ I have too much to do and not enough time to do it.

■ I don't know what to do in a given situation.

■ I loan money to friends and they don't repay it.

■ A friend tells a shared secret to others, or betrays me.

■ _____

■ _____

■ _____

The Stress Cycle

When one event leads to another, it can begin a cycle of stress. When you become overloaded with stress, you are more likely to feel overwhelmed and out of control. *You* control your response to stress.

Read the following story about how 16-year-old Rob coped with his day. As you read it, think about whether many of the things that happened to Rob have happened to you on your bad days. How did one unfortunate event lead to another? Could Rob have prevented some of his problems? How? What coping strategies could he have used to help him better manage his day?

Rob's Day:

1. It's Wednesday. Rob sets his alarm for 7:00 a.m. but it fails to go off. He awakens at 7:35. Because Rob is running late, he skips breakfast, forgets to feed the dog, and doesn't make his bed.

2. Rob dashes for the bus stop, but because he is late, he misses it. Luckily for Rob, his father hasn't left for work. Rob asks for a ride to school. Reluctantly, his father agrees to take him. Since this will take his father out of his way he, too, will be late and he is annoyed at Rob because this is the second time this week that Rob has missed the bus. They ride to school in silence. This makes Rob painfully aware of how unhappy his father is with him.

3. Because Rob arrives late to school, he must go to the office to get a late-pass before he can be admitted to class. Suddenly, Rob remembers that because his father was in a bad mood, he didn't ask his father to write out an explanation for the tardiness. Afraid to call his father, and because he can't get a pass, Rob must sit out first-hour in the office.

4. Because he had no pass and was absent from first-hour class, Rob missed the science test. His teacher says he will not allow Rob to make up the test since he had an unexcused absence. Rob is really upset by this because he needed that test to improve upon his grade point average in order to keep his eligibility for the tennis team. He is the captain of the team and being removed because of low grades will be an embarrassment. Besides, his dad had promised to contribute half of the money for a car if Rob's grades improve by the end of this semester. Thinking about not being able to purchase a car makes Rob angry.

5. Rob goes to his locker to get his books for second-hour class. He can't find his math book. His lockermate has inadvertently picked up Rob's book instead of his own. Rob is frantic. When Rob failed to turn in his math assignment yesterday, his teacher warned him not to let it happen again. Now this overdue math paper is in the book his lockermate has. Rather than face the teacher, Rob decides to skip math class today.

6. Rob's math teacher takes attendance and because Rob's name is not reported on the absence list, the vice-principal calls his mother at work to tell her Rob is not in school.

7. The bell rings and Rob heads off to third-hour class. When friends tease him about his whereabouts during second-hour, he is rude to them. Being upset with his friends makes him feel uneasy.

8. Rob is standing in the lunch line when he notices his lockermate. "Hey Johnson! You took my math book, you idiot!" Rob calls out. Barney Johnson isn't having such a hot day either, and he calls Rob a bad name. Already at the end of his rope, and no longer able to cope, Rob shoves his lockermate against the wall, ready to hit him when he is stopped by the vice-principal, who is surprised to see Rob. The vice-principal tells Rob about the call he made earlier to his mother.

9. Feeling really frustrated, Rob gives the vice-principal a piece of his mind. This gets him into even more serious trouble!

10. As he is being led to the office, Rob thinks about the phone call the vice-principal made to his mother. Knowing his mother has been told he's not in school makes him feel even more anxious. He knows she will call his father. Rob asks if he can use the phone in the office to call his mom, but is reminded that students cannot use the office phone. Rob is not allowed to leave the office now that he's in trouble for fighting, so he can't call her from the pay phone in the hall.

11. Finally, at 3:15 p.m., the school day is over.

Rob had a pretty tense day. Of course, you could write your own stress cycle script using events from your own life. Everyone has bad days, but notice how one event seemed to lead to another. What happens to you when an unpleasant event occurs and you aren't able to get in control or stop other events from following? Can you see, as in the example with Rob, how each event influences and often provokes the next one? What can you do? Understanding how one event leads to another is the first step in coping. You can minimize the harmful effects of stress by learning ways to effectively cope.

The more we understand our students, the better we are able to lead, inspire, and teach our students.

Discussion

1. Describe your students. What is the psychology for the grade level you teach?

2. Identify the stressors that keep students from learning, from developing close friendships with other students, and from developing better relationship with teachers and parents? What are you doing to lessen unproductive stress?

3. How can you identify insecurities and fears in your students, especially older students who put up a brave front? Should you try to get your students to open up?

4. When a child comes to school, he transfers parental bonding to the teacher. In your experiences as an educator, how have you seen this played out?

Chapter 7

IDENTITY:
Helping Students Answer
the "WHO AM I?" Question

When students feel physically safe and emotionally secure, they can focus time, energy, and concentration on the next phase of selfhood — the question of personal identity and essence (the "Who am I?" question). Identity is the third vital ingredient of self-esteem.

There is a beautiful poem called "The Paint Brush" by Lee Ezell that goes like this:

The Paint Brush

I keep my Paint Brush with me, wherever I may go
in case I need to cover up,
so the Real Me doesn't show.
I'm so afraid to show you Me; afraid of what you'll do;
you might laugh, or say mean things;
I'm afraid I might Lose you.
I'd like to remove all my Paintcoats,
to show you the real, true Me.
But I want you to try and understand:
I need you to Like what you see.
So, if you'll be patient and close your eyes,
I'll strip off my coats real slow;
Please understand how much it hurts,
to let the Real Me show.
Now my coats are stripped off. I feel naked, bare and cold.
If you still love me, with all that you see,
you are my friend, pure as gold.
I need to save my Paint Brush, though, and hold it in my hand.
I want to keep it handy, in case somebody doesn't understand.
So please protect me, my dear friend,
and thanks for loving me True;
But, please let me Keep My Paint Brush with me,
Until I love <u>Me</u> too!

— *Lee Ezell*
(Reprinted with permission)

Have you ever felt the earnest apprehension this poem poignantly illustrates? Most of us have. For children, however, such apprehension is ever-present. Parents, teachers, coaches, and friends each expect different things from children. Parents expect good behavior, teachers expect scholastic achievement, and coaches demand superior athletic performance. With so many expectations to meet, a child may wonder, "Who am I? What do *I* want?" How a student sees himself, and how he thinks others view him determines what he will reveal to us.

Why a Student's Image of Himself Influences His Actions

We all have an identity. The question is what do we see ourselves as, and is this image healthy and positive? All too often, a student believes his personal price tag reads "damaged goods" instead of "valuable merchandise." The child who has been physically or emotionally mistreated — or hurt or abandoned by those he is dependent upon and loves — often underestimates himself, or conversely, he exaggerates his self-worth as a way of compensating for low self-opinion. Consequently, his inner picture of himself is out of focus. Sometimes this inner picture needs only minor repair such as fine-tuning or refocusing; sometimes it needs to be replaced with a new, more positive image because the old one creates so many problems.

Accurate or innaccurate, a student's inner picture of her self-worth influences her actions.

Accurate or inaccurate, healthy or dysfunctional, a student's inner picture of her self-worth influences her actions. A student who sees herself in a positive light acts positively, while a student who sees herself as a "problem" child is usually in trouble. A student's perceptions of her capabilities become the baseline for her performance. A student's *self-description* affects her learning potential.

Identity "Windows": The Actual, Ideal, and Public Selves

Answering the "Who Am I?" question means looking at ourselves through three separate "windows" and assessing what we see. These three "windows" are called the *actual*, *ideal*, and *public* selves and they provide us with self-perceptions that help us judge who we are.

The **actual self** is a composite picture of how successful the child feels in each of his many roles as student, friend, son, daughter, brother, sister, paperboy, babysitter, and so on. The actual self reflects the child's overall picture of how he interacts in each of these roles, and how he is greeted in each of them in return. For example, he may feel successful as a student, but not very comfortable with his ability to make and sustain friends. He may feel good about his ability to make friends, but inadequate in his role as a student.

The **ideal self** is made up of the child's aspirations — his *ideal* of how he would like to be and who he wants to become. Aspirations form the basis of such thoughts as, "I wish I were prettier, friendlier, an A-student, thinner, heavier, smarter." Sometimes aspirations are more concrete such as, "I want to be a member of the baseball team, be a lifeguard, be rich and famous . . ." The ideals summed up by statements such as, "When I'm rich . . ." or "When I'm grown up . . . ." represent the child's belief in someday having or being those things.

The **public self** is the aspect of himself that the child is willing to show to others. The public self puts up a good front, or discloses only certain things to others. Sometimes a child is influenced by what others want him to be, or by what he perceives others want.

We all form our own inner pictures of ourselves as we look through these three windows. The key is that our inner picture needs to have a balanced perspective. Ideally, all three aspects are equally balanced. When there are great discrepancies in the overall balance, emotional stress increases. Students who project only their public selves easily lose sight of how the other areas contribute to a healthy self-image.

An example of the distortion caused by depending primarily on the public self can be seen in the story of the late actor and comedian John Belushi. Belushi's public self was that of a clown and a slob, similar to the character he played in the film *Animal House*. Belushi seemed to be just another happy, exuberant guy, rather crass and insensitive. The public accepted him as such. However, the public was less willing to accept him as a sensitive, romantic man. When Belushi tried to play a suave hero in the film *Continental Divide*, he was a flop. Like most of us, Belushi probably believed he had more to offer than slapstick. It must have been very difficult for him to realize the public could accept him as a clown, but that the clownish image was difficult to alter. No one would look past the buffoon to see the intelligence and caring. Belushi's self-identity became more and more tied up in one "self-window," to the exclusion of others. A toll, whether in inappropriate behavior, drugs, depression, or anything else, is exacted for having an out-of-balance life.

When these three aspects of identity are out of balance, a student ends up in turmoil. If she acts primarily from her public self, she may think she has to be popular. She may go too far to please others in a desperate attempt to achieve her goal. Her actions primarily are focused on gaining attention and feedback from others, but deep inside, the message she gives herself is, "No one cares what I want." Consequently, destructive coping strategies such as passive/aggressive behavior often occur. Even if the results are negative, a student strives to resolve inner turmoil.

> Even if the results are negative, a student strives to resolve inner turmoil.

Helping Your Students Build a Positive Sense of Identity

You can help each student develop a healthy self-description. You'll want to start by getting a sense of how *the student sees himself* in order to see how his actual, ideal and public selves differ. Here are some other steps you can take to help build a positive sense of selfhood:

1. Ask students to describe themselves. Design both writing and speaking experiences for your students that allow them to self-disclose. Choose open ended questions such as these: "What four words best describe *you?*" "How do you see yourself?" "What four words best describe how you would *like* to be?" "What are your strengths?" "What do you do really well?" "What do you want to do better?" "How do you think others see you?" "If others were to describe you, what would they say?" Young people enjoy talking and writing about these things, and consider this to be a sign of sincere interest on your part.

2. Be a positive role model. Modeling is the way most of us learn, especially children. Parents and educators are powerful models for young people. Actions always speak louder than words. Don't say, "That's different, I'm an adult," or "Do as I say, not as I do," or "I don't have to stay in shape, I'm the Coach." Children act based on what they see and hear. If you tell your students that you want them to be prepared for tests and complete all their homework, then make certain their tests and papers are graded and returned to them at the time you've promised. This is positive modeling. Remember, our values always show up in our actions!

Our values show up in our actions.

3. Be positive and verbalize the benefits. Verbalize the self-esteem values you want your students to embrace. If you think of yourself in a negative way ("I'm *just* a teacher."), your students will, too. If your outlook is optimistic, your students will have a more positive outlook, too. Show your students the connection between how good you feel about yourself and the positive outcomes. Tell students how your good attitude affects your day. Verbalize "what if" scenarios so students can hear the difference: "Hmmm, I wonder what will happen if I stay in this good mood all day? Will I accomplish more and have a better time?" By verbalizing the benefits of a healthy identity, you teach each student that *he can be in charge* of his attitude.

4. Speak positively about yourself and others. When you speak positively about yourself, your colleagues, your school, your children at home, and your students, you impart the message that self-respect matters. Your students hear you say, "I had a great day, today," and they are more likely to say they had a good day, too. When they hear you say, "I feel good about myself because I managed to stay with the job and get it completed, even though it was really tough," they are more likely to say, "I did a good job handling Frank's teasing me about being short." When students hear, "I was feeling frustrated so I took a walk to calm down and get back in a better mood," they are more likely to say, "I thought I was going to get into a fight but I talked myself out of it."

5. Teach students that they can be in charge. Each student needs to learn that he is responsible, that he determines his outlook, and that he can create his reality. Point out that everyone has bad days and that we don't have to feel as though we have no control over our lives. When you feel you're wasting time because you're in a bad mood, say out loud, "Wait a minute. I'm letting my problem affect everything around me, but I don't need to, and I won't." This shows students that we all "lose it" now and then. When the problem is resolved, students see it was solved in part because you believed in yourself. You improved a bad situation — and they can do the same. Teaching students effective self-management skills helps them learn to cope effectively. Books such as *A Stress Management Guide for Young People* are designed for this purpose. The reference section at the back of this book lists a number of resources for teaching students self-management skills. You may wish to ask the school counselor or librarian for additional suggestions.

The Importance of a Student's Appearance

Appearance is another important part of a student's self-concept. You may say, "What's inside is what counts," but to students, appearance is an important part of identity. Even their perception of physical traits affects their self-perception. This begins at an early age. Children begin to form a concept of themselves and others based on outer beauty, and to differentiate between what they consider to be attractive and unattractive at about 3 years. Children actually stereotype others on the basis of physical attractiveness. Attractive children are looked at, smiled at, touched, and are asked to play and named as "best friends" more often than other children.

Children stereotype others on the basis of physical attractiveness.

Teachers define attractive as a generally neat and clean appearance. An attractive child is clean and wears clean, well-matched clothes. These children receive the most positive numbers of eye contacts by teachers, and garner the most positive strokes and reinforcements in the classroom. Such children receive a good share of positive attention, a plus in helping them cope with the normal frustrations of learning. Studies on the psychology of teaching reveal that teachers call on attractive children more often than unattractive children. Consequently, these children tend to feel better about themselves. Positive attention, touching, and verbal and nonverbal affirmations encourage students to become over-achievers — just as the lack of positive affirmations contributes to underachievement! Don't keep this information from parents. They need to know how they "set the child up" to have positive school experiences.

How the Stages of Growth and Development Influence a Student's Perception of Self

As I travel around the country and speak to youth groups, I frequently ask, "Who are *you*? How would you describe yourself?" Students of all ages automatically describe their physical appearance: "I'm five-foot-six and have green eyes and brown hair." When I ask, "If you could change anything about you, what would it be?," most children, regardless of age, cite some physical characteristic such as, "I wouldn't want to be so tall or short," and so on.

Another aspect of identity is based on a child's perception of his physical self. During childhood, we all undergo the most dramatic stages of growth and development we will experience in our lives. Students are painfully aware of their physical selves as compared to other students, and they judge whether they are "normal" or not by what they see. As children grow and develop, the body has several growth spurts. At times these changes are minor: An 8-year-old girl may gain four to seven pounds and grow three to four inches within a 12- to 14-month period. The 8-year-old boy will gain five to six pounds and gain two to three inches of height. Sometimes these changes are dramatic: The 13-year-old girl will gain, on the average, 14 to 25 pounds, and grow about three to five inches in height during a 12-month period; the 15-year-old boy will gain between 10 and 15 pounds, and gain 10 to 22 inches in height. Each year of life brings about its own set of growth demands. Such changes create a new self-image for the child.

Each year of life brings about its own set of growth demands.

Hormones Have a Life of Their Own!

In addition to outer features of physical growth, organs enlarge and mature in their functioning, and hormones are released, triggering body development and maturity. Added to this are chemical changes in the brain that produce their own behavioral side-effects. Children feel these changes inwardly, but they compare themselves to others outwardly. With each stage of growth and development, a "new" — and not always improved! — child emerges. As Becky, a ninth-grader in Michigan, said to me, "Will the *real* me please stand up and stay around for longer than a few months! I can't keep up with these constant [body] changes, and I'm not so sure I can handle my constantly changing moods, either!"

Helping Students Develop a Healthy Sense of Self

Here are some things you can do to help students develop a healthy attitude about their changing physical selves:

1. Stress the importance of health, wellness, and fitness. Young people need to learn to respect their bodies and care for their health. One way to help students develop a healthy sense of physical identity is to teach the importance of fitness and wellness, and how to achieve and maintain good health. Knowledge about nutrition, exercise, rest, and relaxation are critical.

2. Enlist the support of parents. When young people hear both their parents and teachers emphasize nutrition (how nutrients sustain brain and body functions) and proper rest (how the amount and quality of rest governs our stamina and affects our moods), they are more likely to listen. Teach parents how to talk about nutrition, rest, exercise, and other health-related topics.

3. Encourage school-wide involvement. Check to see what physical education and health courses are provided at your school. Are your programs non-existent or state-of-the-art? For example, Will Baker at Saddleback Valley Unified School District in Mission Viejo, California, heads up an exemplary program where each child's overall health is evaluated at the beginning of each school term. The evaluation assesses inner health — such as cardiovascular fitness — as well as outer health such as a record of the child's caloric intake. Parents are given a copy of the evaluation, along with suggestions for helping their child learn how to safely get in and stay in shape. Each year, the school updates its health-and-fitness profiles on each child in order to track and monitor the child's health throughout his school years.

4. Help students gain insight into their particular stage of growth and development. Young people need to understand more about growth and development, particularly during times of dramatic growth and development. Self-knowledge helps prevent many destructive behaviors. For example, seventh and eighth grade girls may be serious offenders in using diet pills. They may engage in bulemic and anorexic behaviors as a way to control normal weight gain. You can imagine why girls might become alarmed. Until puberty, there is only a slight change in growth and weight gain from year to year, then all at once there is a dramatic gain. You and I look at this student and see an adolescent. She looks in the mirror and asks, "How did I become so 'fat and ugly' so fast?" Her perception is negative. A negative reaction to this normal part of growing up occurs when a girl is not emotionally ready for these dramatic changes. Consequently, she has a "perception warp" of the image she sees in the mirror. Unless she learns to understand why her body is changing so rapidly, she may attempt self-destructive measures aimed at controlling her weight.

Young people need to understand more about their growth and development.

5. Help students gain self-acceptance. Self-knowledge provides understanding. Physical attributes influence a child's thinking about himself, and others. Our culture places an enormous emphasis on outward physical appearance. Physical sex appeal is marketed as a desirable, even mandatory, goal. Millions of dollars are spent each year on promoting one product over the other in giving more sex appeal. Discuss the importance of being oneself. We can't all — and shouldn't want — to be Madonnas!

6. Talk about the importance of appearance. Clothes do count. Students who do not dress like the other children, including those who are overdressed in comparison with other students, feel different and have more negative feelings about themselves. That's why so many private schools request that students wear a uniform, and why many public schools have dress codes. Dressing alike puts students on an equal footing in this one area. Teach parents the importance of a student's "uniform." Suggest they ask themselves these questions:

- When was the last time I observed my child at school with his peers?
- How does my child's overall appearance compare to that of other classmates?
- Is my child clean and well-groomed each day?
- Have I imposed unfair restrictions?
- Is my child overdressed?
- How does my child feel about his appearance?
- How would my child say others describe his appearance?

Asking parents to make sure their child looks like the other children doesn't demand a big emphasis on clothes, but rather, that parents make sure their child is neat and clean and feels good about his appearance. Also, reassure children that they don't need exciting "packaging" to be liked and accepted. Students need to accept themselves and have a realistic sense of selfhood so that not all of their self-perceptions come from their physical being.

When a child possesses self-knowledge, he is friends with the face in the mirror. He is less likely to belittle himself and sell himself short. He's able to "knock and find somebody (himself) home."

Discussion

1. How do your students *group* themselves? How many are "jocks, party animals, brains, nerds," and so on? What effect does belonging to a particular group have on the student's identity? What "identity" is needed to be a member of each group?

2. How differently do your students see you from how you see yourself? Is the different perspective healthy or detrimental?

3. Think of a student who has recently undergone a change of appearance (lost weight, dyed hair). How has his or her sense of self changed, and how has this affected his or her behavior and school performance?

4. Think of a student whose sense of identity is based on a negative image. How can you help him change it? How can you help him create a new — and positive — paradigm?

Chapter 8

IDENTITY:
A Student's Search for Self

Another aspect of the "Who am I?" question has to do with wanting to feel unique, special, and different from others, while simultaneously needing others to see whether your own sense of emerging self is met with acceptance. Feedback is important. *A child's self-concept is the single most important factor in determining his response to peer pressure.* A student with a poorly constructed self-identity is easily influenced by others. Not believing in himself, he often conforms to or mimics his peers, and uses negative statements when describing himself and others. Lacking confidence, he is overly dependent on others and is all too anxious to please them. He may misbehave in order to attract attention. He is uncomfortable with praise, and is likely to deny wrongdoings for fear of rejection. Frequently, he goes out of his way to be different, for example, dressing to extremes to draw attention.

> **A child's self-concept determines his response to peer pressure.**

Students with a healthy self-identity express their individuality without alienating others. They're comfortable accepting praise, and they make positive statements about themselves and others. They stand up for themselves. In the presence of peers using drugs, for example, a student with a healthy self-identity may say, "Hey, I don't do that stuff," or something else that conveys he's not going to participate, and he stays committed to his decision without putting others down or judging them. He isn't easily swayed. He thinks for himself.

How Influential Are You in Your Students' Lives?

A student's first perceptions of himself comes from his parents, and then from you, his teacher. Some educators question just how much influence they have, especially with the child who has had a rough childhood, or has experienced failure after failure in the school setting. After all, students come to school to conquer the curriculum, but they bring emotional baggage along.

Children who have a rough life need even more esteem-building than students who have a stable background. For many emotionally or physically abused students, educators are the best thing going in their lives. Even when a student responds in a negative way, your positive actions are still needed, although that doesn't mean they will be welcomed. Often, when a student hears at home that he is useless, a poor student, or other negative messages, he believes it. When you tell him he is capable, valuable, and worthwhile, those statements don't match his perception, and because they don't, he will respond to his teachers in a negative way. "Oh really," his actions say. "You think I'm okay? Well what about now?" And he shows you his very worst side, challenging you to believe he's okay.

If you expect the student to be well-mannered and capable, and compliment him when he is, he will think of himself as well-mannered and capable. On the other hand, if you tell him he's not, he will believe he isn't. Either way, it's a self-fulfilling prophecy. Children are extremely intuitive. They not only understand what you say, but they are good at reading your body language, too! Each student can sense your attitude toward him, and it influences how he feels about himself. The way you treat him, as well as what you say, influences his sense of self. You believe all students are special; do they believe you believe it?

How "Special" Do You Make Your Students Feel?

Students want teachers to recognize what is going on in their emotional lives.

How do you help students feel their uniqueness? Take a moment to ponder this question. What are the things you say and do that build this important sense of self? Students say that their teachers do it best when we recognize and take notice of what is going on in their emotional lives, such as when we acknowledge that they are in a good or bad mood. Little things do count. "Feeling special" is often an internal response to subtle nuances of tone and word choice. Consider the effect when you say, "Your S.A.T. is on Saturday. Let's take our chapter test the week after, so that you aren't so inundated with work next week," or "The next school baseball game is Thursday at 4:00, and three of you are playing, and I'm sure the rest of you will want to attend. Would you like me to schedule your unit final for tomorrow, or Wednesday so that you have that evening free to enjoy the game without having to worry about preparing for the test the very next day?" The little things we do to show students that we know what's going on increases their feelings of being important. Here are other ways to make students feel *special*:

1. Tell your students that they are special to you. "I enjoy your friendship so much, John." "I can always count on you, Michael." "I'm happy that you are in *my* class." "I really like this class. You are a great bunch of kids!"

2. Talk about *why* you're happy to be their teacher. Don't give your class the feeling that teaching is a chore and they are a burden to be endured. Don't make them feel as if they are a bunch of misfits, or that you're simply stuck with them. Remember, students live up to your expectations. They respond to your attitudes about them. You want them to feel special and worthy: The more difficult the class, the more you need to search for ways of improving their *class image*.

3. Go the extra mile. Help each student feel good about his strengths, but help him understand we all have weaknesses, too. Show tolerance and patience as he struggles to make sense of areas that create learning blocks for him. Go the extra mile as he struggles. When you have a student who is struggling with a concept and she gets a poor test paper back, she needs your support. Say something like, "Kerri, I can see that you're working really hard and you're struggling. Why don't you come in tomorrow noon and I'll bring my lunch and we'll see if we can try this one more time. I want to be sure I'm teaching this in a way that you can understand. Even though this paper is an F, I don't want you to get discouraged. Let's work together on this; I really want to help you. Does that sound like a good plan to you?"

4. Encourage students to take pride in their achievements, both great and small. Experiences are personal. Children must enjoy and be proud of their own accomplishments, and should not always depend on others for approval. Teach the value of self-satisfaction. Help students turn "teacher-pleasing" behavior into goals for themselves.

Teach the value of self-satisfaction.

5. Teach students to respect themselves. Teach students to value themselves as people and not try to be someone else. Encourage students to explore and appreciate their own talents, interests, and ideas. Help them to accept and learn from mistakes and not overreact to them. Show them how to accept successes and failures. Teach that each of us must be our own best friend. Teach the importance of spending time by themselves to examine their own thoughts and feelings. Encourage them to get involved in activities they can enjoy by themselves, such as reading or other hobbies.

TEACHING STUDENTS TO STAND UP FOR THEMSELVES

You can help your students develop a stronger sense of identity by helping them clarify and sharpen their "self-picture." There are a number of skills to help students learn this. A good place for you to begin is by teaching students assertiveness skills — to confront others with assertiveness.

Assertive Choice

Assertiveness skills teach students how to assert their rights without intimidating others or being intimidated by them. Young people need effective communication skills and assertive training to enable them to convey their feelings and opinions to others. Yelling or arguing rarely convinces anyone, nor can others "read minds" and guess what someone wants or needs. Being nice to people doesn't guarantee that they'll be nice in return. To have their needs met, students must learn how to communicate what their needs are. Help students to develop assertiveness skills so they can confidently confront situations that typically produce anxiety and frustration, or cause them to deny their feelings.

As you no doubt have learned from experience, not all students have a problem asserting themselves! Some students learn that by shouting, pouting, ridiculing, and bullying others they can get what they want. Other students learn to be the sweet, likable "I'll-do-anything-you-want" type in order to get others to respond the way they want. Help students learn how to assert themselves *appropriately*. To be

An assertive manner is direct, self-respecting and straightforward.

assertive means to value yourself and to act with confidence and authority.

Assertiveness is "owning" the responsibility to achieve what you need, and not giving the responsibility for that ownership to someone else. Assertiveness is communicating so others will listen and not be offended. Assertiveness gives others the opportunity to respond in return. An assertive manner is direct, self-respecting, and straightforward, not rude, pushy, or bossy. The following verbal and nonverbal "cues" represent assertive behavior.

- **Eye contact.** The assertive child makes direct eye contact with you. This doesn't mean he stares you down without blinking. It means he looks you in the eye and holds eye contact throughout most of the conversation.

- **Hand gestures.** He uses hand gestures to emphasize the content and importance of what he says.

- **Posture.** Posture also indicates assertiveness. Sitting or standing straight when communicating, shoulders back, head up are examples of assertive body language.

- **Voice.** Assertive children speak up and do not mumble. They do not weaken assertive statements by dropping or raising their voice at the end of a statement, turning it into a question. Nor do they make an assertive statement, then follow it with an "Okay?" before the listener has time to respond. Assertive children avoid a whiny tone and do not hesitate in their speech by using fillers such as "you know." Assertive children know when to *stop* talking.

- **Owning your statements.** One hallmark of assertive behavior is the making of "I" statements, such as: "I feel . . .," "I like . . .," "I wish . . .," "I would appreciate . . .," "I need . . ." The passive person gives the responsibility to someone else, often finishing a statement by asking, "Don't you think so?" or "Is that okay?"

By teaching students how to assert their needs, they learn to communicate in a direct and straightforward fashion. They learn the benefits of personal power — and that other people respect honesty and can accept criticism if it's presented in an open, honest, and kind way. Statements that affirm what the student is feeling and what he needs are one way a student learns a sense of identity and takes responsibility for himself.

Assessing Student Assertiveness

How good are your students at communicating their needs? Do they let others know how they're feeling? Here are some questions to test their ability to stand their ground. Discuss these questions with your students, and ask them to respond in a writing assignment.

1. A girl asks to cut in front of you in a line. You don't want to let her cut. What do you do or say?

2. A classmate asks to copy your class assignment. You don't want him to. What do you do or say?

3. The teacher asks the entire class to stay after school because someone was talking. You don't want to take the blame for something you know isn't your fault. What do you do?

4. What can you do if another student is calling you names?

5. You don't understand a problem the teacher has just explained. What would you say in asking for help?

6. Your mother is in the car honking the horn for you to hurry so she can get you to school. You still need to feed and water your dog. What should you do?

7. Your teacher has returned your homework, and you notice that she has marked an answer wrong that you are sure is correct. What do you say or do?

8. You really like one of your classmates, but another classmate tells you not to "hang around" (for younger students, "play") with her because she is "weird." What do you do or say?

9. You trip and fall. Someone calls you clumsy. What do you do or say?

10. You agree to meet a friend to ride bikes to school and you forget. What do you do? What do you say to your friend when you see him?

11. A student calls you a jerk! What do you do or say?

12. Someone says you lied when you didn't. What do you do or say?

13. You throw a ball and it hits someone. What do you do or say?

As adults, we periodically pause and take stock of ourselves. We ask ourselves "Who am I?" "How have I changed through the years?" "What am I up to?" The question of "Who am I?" looms large for children, too.

Educators play a key role in helping each student feel that she is special and valued. When we show acceptance, encourage pride and help her to trust her feelings and respect herself, we pave the way for developing a stronger sense of selfhood and for helping her to clarify and sharpen her self-picture.

Discussion

1. How does a student's low or positive self-image contribute to his role as a learner?

2. How do you deal with a child who acts arrogant? Passive? Aggressive? Shy?

3. Do you feel *you* are special to your students? How do your students show you that you are special? How does that feeling affect your behavior towards them?

Chapter 9

AFFILIATION:
The Student's Need for Adult Friendships

"People who need people are the luckiest people in the world," as Barbara Streisand sang in a popular song, touches on the uniquely human need to be with others. Affiliation, or a sense of belonging, is our deep-seated desire to be with others. When we interact with others we learn as much about ourselves as we do about them.

Most of us seek out the company of others and long to be accepted by them. We especially need to feel accepted by those we consider important to us. Children need adults in their lives before they need peers. Children learn to depend on others — the adults in their lives — before they learn to be independent. As adults, we teach children to be independent, yet we also want them to understand that they share a connection with others — they must realize that other people matter. In short, a sense of interdependence, a healthy sense of mutual reciprocity, is the ideal. Whether you call this need to belong "socialization," "friendship," or "peer pressure," it serves a purpose. Being with others gives us another glimpse of our own human need for warmth, caring, and connection.

When we feel that others accept us and want to be with us, we're more likely to care about them in return. Students with high self-esteem will more consistently offer help and behave more responsibly toward other students than will low self-esteem peers. Unfortunately, not all students have a solid sense of belonging. Of the more than one million adolescent girls who become pregnant each year, 85 to 95% elect to keep their babies rather than give them up for adoption because they believe that a baby will provide the kind of love and acceptance parents and teachers have not. Studies from the Center for Educational Statistics on school dropouts clearly substantiate that a feeling of being "unaffiliated" — of not belonging — is the second leading cause of leaving school before graduation.

A feeling of not belonging is the second leading cause of dropping out of school.

We know that young people who do not feel they belong are more likely to:

■ have difficulty making and keeping friendships,

■ be easily influenced by others,

■ be low achievers in school,

■ be uncomfortable working in group settings,

- isolate themselves from others and become even more lonely,
- depend on behaviors such as bullying, showing-off, being uncooperative, withdrawing, ridiculing, and being insensitive to the needs of others,
- experience learning difficulties,
- be identified as juvenile delinquents,
- plan a pregnancy because they want "someone to love,"
- drop out of school, or
- experience mental health problems in adulthood.

In contrast to young people with a sense of belonging, they are able to:
- initiate new friendships,
- show sensitivity toward others,
- cooperate and share with others,
- more easily achieve peer acceptance and be sought out by others,
- feel valued by others,
- express happiness, and
- excel in school.

The Five Adults Children Want and Need Most in Their Lives

Indeed, parents are the most important people in a child's life. I find many parents are surprised to learn just *how* important they are to their children, especially as children grow older and seek the friendships of others. Yet, when children are asked to list the five most meaningful people in their lives, both girls and boys name parents as No. 1. While the first person they list is a parent, the second person they name is most generally the *other* parent, sometimes even in cases of separation or divorce.

Teachers often are chosen as the child's third and fourth most important person in life.

Third place goes to a favorite teacher — the teacher the student considers to be the "best listener." Other choices for the third place include stepparent, school custodian, bus driver, or an educator the child develops a liking for but who may not be directly in an instructional role with the student. The fourth person named is the teacher whose teaching style matches the child's learning style and who, with persistence, encourages the student to develop his strengths, interests, and aptitudes.

In fifth place, girls list their grandmother, followed by a sibling (male or female), and anyone else who might serve as a support system. Boys list an uncle, a grandfather, followed by a sibling (brothers are listed first). Peers rarely show up in the top five until children are 15-and-a-half years or older.

Why do you think that's so? The answer is that peers, for the most part, are *situational friends*. A friend is often chosen for convenience — because the two are neighbors, or because they share a locker or a class together, or they are on the same team, or get assigned to do a special project, or because they sit beside each other in class. Such friendships rarely last long. Some last only a few months. This doesn't mean that when friendships end they are painless. Children experience much hurt and turmoil when friendships break up. During the course of childhood many friendships will be formed and then abandoned. The *influence* of friends and peers (these two are different) is closely tied to the process of socialization, of learning how to interact with others. Unfortunately, nearly 37% of elementary school children are not named as a friend by anyone in their class, and 29% receive no nomination from anyone in the school setting.

Many parents and teachers erroneously believe that a student's friends are more important to him than his relationships with adults. Healthy relationships with adults are crucial — when adults are physically or emotionally distant from a child, only then does the child turn to peers for acceptance and belonging. Not belonging is a lonely experience and children instinctively try to alleviate the pain they feel. This is when peer groups become the most influential, and potentially the most dangerous. In the absence of parents, teachers, or other significant adults, most children will pay almost any price to belong. As you have no doubt found out, these days there are very few Mrs. Cleavers at home cooking dinner in high heels and pearls, with a father and husband who knows best! Given the erratic lifestyle of so many households, as well as parents who are often permissive and who do not set well-defined boundaries for behavior, educators have become an even greater source of stability for children.

In the absence of significant adults, the child will pay almost any price to belong.

Where Have All the Parents Gone?

As educators, we need to urge parents to spend quality and quantity time with their children. A lack of *quality* time spent with parents is the No. 1 reason why so many youth are unhappy. It's been estimated that, on the average, parents spend less than five minutes each day engaged in fruitful conversation with their age 4- to 18-year-old children. Significant conversations are different than, "Did you take out the garbage?" "Did you get your homework done?" "Did you make up your bed?" or "Did you feed the dog?" Children need special bonding time that develops their personal and emotional well-being.

At a recent seminar I conducted for parents and teens, a mother and her daughter sat together several rows from the front. At one point, the mother raised her hand and said to me, "My 16-year-old has her own phone line, a TV and a stereo in her room, and closets full of the latest clothes. She's still not happy. Instead, she's rebellious and defiant. What's her problem?"

To break the heaviness of the moment, I turned to her 16-year-old daughter sitting next to her and said, "Well, what *is* your problem?"

"My mother!" she shot back instantly. After the laughter died down, the teenager added, "Well, she just doesn't care about *me*."

"Why do you say that?" I asked. "What does she do or not do that gives you that feeling?"

"Well," the daughter said, now speaking in a tone that revealed both pain and frustration, "I've been a cheerleader for eight football games, and so far she hasn't been to one of the games to see me. And when my History teacher scheduled a conference with her, she didn't show up. She doesn't really care about me."

"Yeah, tell me about it!" chimed in a boy a few seats over. "My dad's always telling me how busy he is whenever I ask him to spend time with me. Last week-end I asked him if he could play catch. He said he didn't have the time, but when his friend called and asked him to go fishing, he was gone in a flash. He'll spend time with any of his friends before he'll spend time with me!"

I'm sure you've heard similar laments from your students. Here are some things *you* can do to help students get their needs met for belonging.

1. Develop relationship-building skills. I want to emphasize how important *your* relationship-building skills are. Your ability to develop relationships with your students is the foundation for developing self-esteem in the classroom. Each student wants to feel special. Show an interest in each student as an individual. Again, students don't care how much you know, until they know how much you care. What are you currently doing to help your students feel connected to you?

Your ability to develop relationships with your students is the foundation for developing self-esteem in the classroom.

2. Give each learner a sense of being special. A busy teacher needs to be both watchful and creative. Noticing a student who has become uncharacteristically quiet, disruptive, or sullen takes vigilance when that student is one among 30 others. Once the reason is discovered it takes creative energy to come up with a solution. For example, if you learned a student can't grasp a particular subject, you need to provide extra time and attention, tutoring or peer tutoring, or you need to supply him with resources to take home and study, or perhaps you might decide to have him tested for a learning disability. To make the wisest decision for each student means understanding each particular student and his needs. If you take the time, the student will know you're interested when he becomes aware that you truly care for him and his progress as an individual.

3. Show acceptance. Your caring and acceptance are vital to helping students feel connected to you. Your actions reflect your acceptance as much as your words do. Here are some ways for you to show acceptance:

■ **Verbal expressions.** Say the words directly — don't simply hint. Make remarks such as: "You're so considerate, Bill," or "I like to have you in class, Mary." From these remarks, children draw conclusions about how connected they are to us, and *how that feels to us*. These statements help students formulate opinions about their strengths and weaknesses such as, "Am I really good at spelling?" "Do others like my ideas?" "Does my teacher really think I'm important?"

■ **Nonverbal expressions.** Your nonverbal expressions are as important as what you say. Your facial expression and body language communicate your caring almost as directly as your words. Remember, students can tell whether there is sincerity or hypocrisy in the air. When you walk around the class, do you stand beside the same few students, or do you treat all students equally? Small actions — body language and facial expressions — speak to students. Make certain your nonverbal expressions are telling students those things you want them to hear.

■ **Empathic listening.** A teacher who is a good listener builds a relationship with his students and sets the foundation for sharing feelings. When we listen, we tell our students they are valuable and worthy of our time and attention. We show empathy when we respond not just to what a student says but to what she feels. Sometimes, a few minutes of your undivided attention tells a student all she wants to know about your acceptance. Your *listening actions* say, "I take you seriously; I care about you."

4. Allow students to be a part of class decisions when appropriate. Consulting with your students shows you value their opinions. They learn that their views are important to you. Students learn to view themselves as competent and worthwhile. Marsha, a 12-year-old girl in Santa Monica, California, said to me, "Our teacher asks our opinion about different things, like about whether we wanted to have a multiple choice or essay quiz; which play we wanted to do for our Christmas program; where we wanted to go on our field trip. And each of our opinions really matters to her. That feels great!" Being allowed to have a part in decisions makes Marsha and her classmates feel that they count, that their teacher considers their input valuable.

Relationship Building Is Central to Self-Esteem

Affiliation, the sense of belonging, is an essential element in building self-esteem. Students know whether you care about them. You build a sense of affiliation by your actions but even more so by your words.

In the teacher's lounge, you probably brag about "your students." It's important to you to feel connected to them. It's even more important for your students to know they have an affiliation with you. By telling and showing students how much you care, and how pleased you are that they are your students, you make them feel special. You help them develop their identity and sense of self as valued and respected individuals.

Have you noticed how some teachers seem to quietly and unassumingly command attention and admiration from their students, while other teachers "get no respect"? Effective educators have learned the importance of establishing rapport with their students, and understand its contribution to their students' desire and ability to learn. When your students feel you care, they are secure, validated, and confident of their intrinsic worth. You make it easy for them to respect you and cooperate with you. Keep in mind that *students don't care how much you know until they know how much you care.*

Unfortunately, just being a teacher no longer commands the respect it once

When your students feel you care, they are secure, validated, and confident of their intrinsic worth.

did. Given that being older, wiser, and a fountainhead of knowledge isn't enough, what can you do to convince and empower your students to be eager learners? Of all the tools to do that, the most influential is to have a positive balance in the "emotional bank account" that you set up with your students.

Opening an "Emotional Bank Account" with Your Students

With each student, you open an *emotional bank account*. The concept works just like your account at the bank. What you do and say can be a deposit, or a withdrawal in the emotional account. Deposits are made through your positive and helpful actions — courtesy, respect, dependability, constancy, fairness, and professional effectiveness. Withdrawals are made through discourtesy, disrespect, putdowns that tear down, emotional distance, poor quality teaching, or papers that are poorly marked. I'm a parent of a 16-year-old. Here's how this principle works for me. My daughter Jennifer's curfew is 11:00 p.m. When I ask that she honor her curfew and be in by that time, I mean it. This curfew is negotiable only in special cases. Mandate or not, should she choose to violate it, she could. That's out of my control, and is completely up to her. How will I get her to honor the curfew or, in unforeseeable circumstances, call me immediately to explain?

Deposits are made through your positive and helpful actions.

The best way is to have her *want* to uphold the curfew because she, too, values our relationship and doesn't want to break the trust she has with me. In other words, I need to have a good relationship with her. More specifically, I should have a "positive balance" in our emotional bank account in order for her to value the curfew. If I have a "negative balance" in my daughter's emotional bank account — if I make promises but do not keep them, for example — then because the trust has been violated, she may make a withdrawal on my emotional account. By being late or by not calling, she knows she causes me worry and anguish. But if I keep making deposits in our emotional bank account, my reserves build up. Her trust in me grows, and I can call on that trust if need be. I can even make a few minor mistakes and still be forgiven. But if I continually make withdrawals from the account without making deposits, the reserve is diminished. If I continue making withdrawals, the emotional bank account becomes overdrawn. At that point, I have little, if any, trust with her. I have to watch every step.

Just as with the parent and child relationship, educators build or deplete emotional bank accounts with their students. For example, Gwen, a ninth-grade student, had a history of arriving late to her first period class. Knowing that Gwen's life was fraught with emotional problems, her teacher, Mrs. Neilson, made a point of ignoring Gwen's loud entrance, and avoided voicing reprimands in front of Gwen's classmates. She simply looked at her and said, "Good morning, Gwen. Please see me after class." Although recognizing Gwen's tardiness as a concern, the teacher also took the time to praise Gwen's efforts on the mornings she did arrive on time. To hold to the boundary of making up time when Gwen was late to class, and to help her *correct* her tardy behavior, Mrs. Neilson spoke to her alone, expressing her concern, and then asked if she could assist Gwen in getting to class on time. Mrs. Neilson's diligent praise, and her consideration shown toward Gwen by speaking to her privately, as well as the obvious caring and concern she demonstrated in this situation, acted as deposits. Few people had treated Gwen with such respect. Inspired to please Mrs. Neilson, Gwen began working harder to get to class on time, and soon she did. The year before, Gwen's teacher had resorted to ridicule, sarcasm, and threats — all withdrawals — and as a result, Gwen had had no desire to make it to her class on time. In fact, she made a scene upon entering, just to annoy the teacher. Because Gwen was used to negative feedback, at first she had difficulty believing Mrs. Neilson would be consistent in her positive approach. As time passed, Gwen realized she could count on Mrs. Neilson to be fair, consistent, and *serious* in her resolve to hold Gwen accountable for getting to class on time, and for her good behavior.

Emotional Bank Accounts Are Fragile but Resilient

Emotional bank accounts are very fragile but, at the same time, very resilient. If I have a large emotional bank account, say an imaginary sum of $1,000 of emotional reserve capacity with my daughter, I can make small withdrawals of $100 from time to time and she will understand and overlook it. For instance, I may need to make a very unpopular, authoritarian decision without even involving her. Let's say that Jennifer wants to attend a three-day camping trip and I'm not feeling comfortable with how the activity will be chaperoned. I may say, "No. You can't go. I will not support this particular activity." She may pout or be angry. And she'll tell me so. My unpopular decision may cost me $100 in her eyes. But if I have a $1,000 bank account and I make a $100 withdrawal, I still have $900 left. In other words, it's unlikely that she will go to her room, pack for the trip, and go anyway, although that is always an option!

I also could try to lessen the amount of the withdrawal. For example, I could explain my reasoning, thus possibly redepositing some portion of the $100. Perhaps I could suggest that she call up a favorite friend and invite her over for a special weekend. I also might offer to pay for the movie rather than keep with my current rule of her using her allowance money for such activities. I might pay for special theater tickets, or allow a curfew later than usual, just to show my willingness to be compassionate about the fact that she isn't where she wants to be. Therefore, I may even get back 20 or 30 "emotional dollars," or some other portion of the original withdrawal.

As an educator, there are times when you have to make up for a "mass withdrawal." For example, Mr. Thorton asked his play practice group to settle down and quit talking. When at least five of his 18 students, still wound up, remained rambunctious and continued talking, Mr. Thorton kept the entire group for 10 minutes. The whole group paid the price for a few students' behavior. You can bet those students who were not talking felt this was a "withdrawal"! The next day, Mr. Thorton explained the reasoning behind his actions and acknowledged its "unfairness." This explanation might earn him back a portion of the amount

> **Emotional bank accounts are very fragile but, at the same time, very resilient.**

withdrawn from each student's emotional bank account. Another way Mr. Thorton could have placed a deposit in his students' account would be to hold the culprits behind the next day while allowing the others to leave 10 minutes early, or other alternatives could be generated to show his empathy.

Do You Contribute to Discipline Problems?

Like my influence with my daughter, Mrs. Neilson's with Gwen and Mr. Thorton's with his students, your influence over each student depends on your individual relationship with each. Maintaining order and an atmosphere conducive to teaching and learning is difficult if you threaten, ignore, ridicule, or putdown, or if you are unfair, harsh, unreasonable, or if you neglect your students' feelings. When your account has a positive balance, learning, achievement, and student happiness are high.

Maintaining order is difficult if you threaten or ridicule your students.

With younger students who may be susceptible to threats and manipulation, you might get what you want through the use of such inappropriate methods. However, older students don't tolerate threats. Regardless of the threats you make (lowering grades, keeping students after school, sending students to the office for discipline, or calling their parents), without a high trust level and mutual respect, your influence over your students is diminished. A lack of deposits leads to an overdrawn emotional bank account, a breakdown in the relationship, and a lack of influence. In short, you have a discipline problem on your hands, and you have contributed to it.

Making Deposits in Your Students' Accounts

Given that the emotional bank account is so important in working effectively with students and in getting students to *learn*, what can you do to build up your account? Making daily "deposits" yields the best dividends. While only you know what works best with each of your classes, these are the basics:

1. Be fair to all students. Call on *all* your students. Certainly, you will have favorite students, but strive to treat all children with courtesy and respect. Believe in all your students. Believe all students have a right to experience success in the classroom. Believe all students can learn. Make eye contact with all students. When you move around the classroom, stand near the quiet, shy students, as well as the bright and friendly ones. Don't neglect to call on a particular student simply because you expect he won't answer your question correctly. Allow each student the same opportunity to feel worthy.

2. Believe in your students. Display patience and don't make judgments without facts and evidence. Some students may seem to be at the center of trouble more than others. Remember, students live up, or down, to the expectations of their teachers. Demonstrating willingness to believe in a student's innocence can be a huge deposit for a student who doesn't expect it from anyone — and it encourages him to prove himself worthy of your trust.

3. Respect your students. I've worked with educators who feel that they're "here to teach, not to coddle." However, showing respect to your students helps them to learn to be respectful of others. Children resent others for not treating them with dignity and respect. Some educators think children should respect educators because they are older, as though age is the primary basis for respect. Age is a valid starting point, but it works both ways — you have to give respect in order to gain respect. When students don't feel respected, they speak out. Consider the student who says, "I'm not staying after class. If you can't figure out who was talking, that's your problem, not mine. It wasn't me and I'm not staying after!" Quite often, such a child is disciplined for the honesty of his accurate observations.

4. Listen emphatically. Listening is powerful because it is a sign of respect. It's also an important way to meet a child's deep need for emotional security. Listening is understanding. Although you may not necessarily agree with the student's opinion, when you listen, you give her the chance to be heard. Listening conveys to the student that her ideas and opinions count. She matters. Her teacher cares about her. Being listened to makes a student feel worthwhile. The next time a student needs to talk to you, observe *your* own listening style. Do you fidget restlessly, or do you show your interest in what he has to say? Look at the student and meet his eyes. Give him your complete attention. Imagine how you would feel if you went to another teacher's room, bursting with big news. You launch into the story, but it's obvious your colleague's attention is wandering. How do you feel? You feel deflated. And you're an adult, aware of your feelings, able to isolate the action (the lack of attentiveness) from the intent — your colleague probably didn't mean to hurt your feelings. Children don't have this perspective. To them, you merely stopped listening. That implies they're not important to you, and that their accomplishment wasn't such a big deal after all. They feel a little less worthy. Do you show *all* students, by listening, that they are valued?

Being listened to makes a student feel worthy.

5. Answer questions and communicate without being condescending. It isn't always easy to ask for help. Imagine how humiliating it is to build up your nerve to ask for help and then to be ridiculed for it. Treating the student's questions and requests for help with respect enables you to make deposits. All interactions, verbal and nonverbal, should be treated with respect. Being respected is how young people learn to respect others.

6. Write personal comments on your student's papers. Every child thrives on attention, encouragement, and praise. Make every effort to provide your students with written comments on their assignments. Of course, your comments should be sincere and your praise deserved, or they will mean little to the student, and they will harm your credibility. When you look for and find ways to give attention and encouragement, you instill both confidence and a sense of worth in your students.

7. Keep your word. Students build their expectations around your demands. If you keep your word, your integrity builds. For example, telling your students you will grade their test and then not doing so is a breach in trust that harms your credibility. If you say you're going to give a quiz, give it! If not, make sure students know why. Your reason for not doing so *is* important. If you say you're going to be at a school function, be there. When you tell a student he will give his report on Wednesday, but Wednesday comes and goes, and although he's prepared, he isn't called on, that student considers your oversight a withdrawal. He counted on doing that report — he probably dressed special for the occasion — plus he spent time and energy to prepare it.

8. Individualize "deposits" when possible. "Deposits" should be very special to the receiver. I remember agonizing over what I would give as a gift to a dear friend of mine who was getting married. As I was shopping in a large department store, several beautiful crystal vases caught my eye. I finally made the decision by reasoning, "If I received one of these beautiful vases, which one would *I* want?" Finally, I chose the one that I would most long to have, but before I purchased it, I invited my friend to lunch at the restaurant in the store where I had seen the vase. After lunch, we browsed a bit, and I deliberately directed our rambling to the department where the vase was located. "Aren't these lovely!" I remarked, intently watching her expression. I wanted, of course, to see if she thought it was as regal as I did.

"Well, I suppose so," she said, sounding quite uninterested. "But I really don't like vases. And to tell the truth, I really don't like flowers all that much. I sure hope I don't end up with a half dozen vases for wedding gifts!" Just as I needed a better understanding of my friend's interests, you need to know what your students value most.

9. Sincerely apologize when you are wrong. You make a deposit when you can sincerely say: "I was wrong. I'm sorry." Students are very forgiving, *when* you acknowledge that you have been unfair. But there's a limit. *You can't talk your way out of something you've behaved your way into.* Apologies lose their meaning when you keep repeating your transgressions. If you embarrass a student in front of his peers, acknowledge it. Say, "John, I'm sorry to have embarrassed you in front of the class the way I did. That was unfair." Such recognition not only reduces the amount of the withdrawal, but becomes a deposit.

The key to having influence with a student is his perception that he can influence you.

Your Credibility Depends on Your Emotional Bank Balance

Remember, the key to having influence with a student is his perception that he can influence you. The attitude of "I want to understand you" is enormously attractive because the student believes you can be influenced. What he says has a chance of being heard and considered. You make it clear you care about your student's interests, concerns, needs, hopes, fears, doubts, and joys. You acknowledge his feelings and understand that his viewpoint might be different than yours. *Know that from every person's point of view, he is right.* You say in a cheerful tone, "Good, you see it differently. I would like to understand how you see it."

This conveys, "I see it differently," rather than, "I'm right and you're wrong." Such language admits, "Like mine, your views and feelings are worth examining. Let's explore them. You matter to me, I want to understand you."

Such transactions lead to healthy teacher-student relationships. Healthy teacher-student relationships build the self-esteem of each student, as well as your own self-esteem.

Discussion

1. A child who feels accepted by and connected to others feels liked, appreciated, and respected. He learns to seek out and maintain friendships. He is able to cooperate and share with others. While maintaining a sense of independence, he learns *inter*dependence — a healthy sense of interrelatedness. This results in his feeling good about his social experiences with family, friends, teachers, and others. In your experiences as an educator, how have you seen this played out?

2. How do you develop affiliation needs for youth in *your* classroom? What else can you do?

3. What activities promote belonging for youth in your school environment? What else needs to be done?

4. What supports a sense of affiliation for colleagues in your school setting? What else needs to be done?

Exercise

Have students write down how many hours a day they think they spend talking to or interacting with their parents, then have them keep a precise time log to see the actual amount of time. Discuss different need levels for parental attention based on previously learned developmental stages.

Chapter 10

BELONGING:
The Student's Need for Peer Friendships

An ancient Chinese proverb says, "A child's life is like a piece of paper on which every passerby leaves a mark," and it's so. A child's *self-perception* is a by-product of the opinions and perceptions of others, including what others say to him and how they treat him. As children win acceptance and experience rejections, they arrive at a verdict about themselves as to just how acceptable and lovable they are to others.

In the early years, a child's primary relationships consist of his family, caretakers, and teachers. In the previous chapter, I discussed how important adults are in helping a child build a sense of affiliation. A sense of belonging is also developed by the child's relationships with other children. When a child's circle of relationships is expanded to include many other children, he learns that to be part of a group demands new skills. A healthy sense of selfhood is necessary for his adjustment into that group. A student with a positive sense of self is more willing to accept others without comparing them to himself or comparing himself to his friends. The low self-esteem student stands back and hopes that someone eventually approaches him. He may stand alone for a long time, then eventually decide that other children don't like him, and become even more of a loner as a result.

> **A student with a positive sense of self shows acceptance of others and joins in making new friends.**

A student who thinks well of herself is more at ease in social situations, while a student who is insecure and considers herself unworthy keeps to herself to avoid the chance of humiliation or rejection. "Popular" students are popular because they know how to make friends and interact with them. Through successful interactions with others, they come to feel appreciated and accepted. The goal is not so much to ensure that each student is popular, as it is to help students gain confidence in social encounters in a healthy *inter*dependent way.

What It Takes to Be a Friend

A student needs an array of interpersonal skills in showing approval and support of others. For example, while participating in the group, the student needs to assert himself as an individual with his own style without alienating others. No doubt about it, learning to be a friend takes practice and a great deal of skill!

Friendships are filled with customs, rituals, and rules, all part of a dance for *acceptance*. Being left out is painful, so many children will go along with anything. But group membership is not automatic, and the rules for belonging are always changing. Rules that worked in the early years of childhood don't work in the upper elementary years. Young children find it easier to make friends — a student who is good at baseball finds acceptance in the sports group. If he has a bicycle, he is part of the street fun. Moving from childhood to adolescence causes real culture shock. During adolescence, the rules even among friends change regularly.

Socialization is not always an easy task for students to learn on their own. Schools must design required courses that help students learn interpersonal and social skills, especially necessary when cultural diversity and language barriers are commonplace in today's schools. This is even more important for students who are bused from their neighborhood into new school settings and then returned home. These students have fewer opportunities to connect. They are outsiders both at school and in their own neighborhood.

Interpersonal relationship problems that arise between youngsters in the school environment account for much down time. When students are in emotional chaos, they are not good learners.

We must design courses to help students learn interpersonal and social skills.

Children Need Skills to Make and Sustain Friendships

Interactions with other children provide the student with yet another view of himself. We instinctively sense this when we talk about the importance of friendships and how much influence they exert in a student's life, yet we rarely teach students about the nature of friendships. Nor do we seem to teach students how to *manage* the persuasive influence that other students exert over them. Before we can teach students how to build and maintain friendships, we must understand the nature of young friendships.

The Nature of a Student's Friendships

Friendships fall into two categories. Students call them the *outsiders*, and the *insiders*.

Outsider friendships are characterized by convenience, availability, and the opportunity to "use" the other in a time of need. Friendship is based primarily on physical proximity, cooperation, and ego fulfillment. Such external friendships are very painful because the unsuspecting child — the one who has been used — feels betrayed when the friendship ends.

■ **Limited physical proximity.** The availability of someone who lives down the street or who is in a child's French class or tumbling class provides a student with outside opportunities based on convenience. This is only a "situational" friendship and rarely does it grow into a satisfying relationship. Suzie, who shared her lunch with Patti, won't even sit at the same table with Patti now that the reading group has changed and they no longer share the same reading group.

■ **Cooperation toward personal goals.** Students form friendships with other children who cooperate with them in their attempts to attain personal goals and rewards. In this friendship, the child has little time for anyone who hinders or contradicts his getting what he wants. It's not uncommon for an aggressive child to develop a friendship for the duration of a project, and then drop the relationship as soon as the project is over. Let's say you select two co-captains for a spelling contest. Whereas 4- to 7-year-olds will choose their best friend (defined as the one sitting next to her that day!), 8- to 12-year-olds will choose the best spellers to be on their team and loyalty extends only until the end of the spelling contest. Most 13- to 15-year-olds will choose children they secretly admire and would love to be near, although this is as close as they'll get! Baffled by the change, the left-behind child doesn't understand what happened. How could he be so "on" only to be so quickly "off"?

■ **Ego fulfillment.** Students often side with those who like them, or those who see them in a positive light and promote them to others. John, for example, may value Jimmy's company because Jimmy is constantly boasting about John's successes. This doesn't guarantee mutual friendship, however, only that the friendship serves the purpose of meeting John's ego needs. Jimmy generally is not treated well inside or outside the relationship. Plus, once the friendship crumbles, Jimmy is devastated. Having relied on reference power — someone else's power to be "somebody" — Jimmy is alone now. Often, the betrayed child is ridiculed by the "friend" who left.

> Often, the betrayed child is ridiculed by the "friend" who left.

Insider friendships are characterized by ample opportunity for togetherness or likeness. Similarities exist in six key areas:

1. **Respect.** The student says, "I'll check with Melody. She'll know what to do."
2. **Trust.** Trust promotes loyalty. "I know I can count on Suzie — she never lets me down."
3. **Understanding.** There is a sense of what is important to each other — they know why a friend does what he does. "I know *why* he's upset."
4. **Enjoyment.** They genuinely enjoy each other's company. "I always feel good when I'm with her."
5. **Acceptance.** They accept each other as they are. "That's just Jim. That's the way he is."
6. **Confiding.** Friends share feelings with each other. "She tells me things that no one else knows about her."

The closer the proximity, the greater amount of information students know about each other. This frequency of interaction provides children with opportunities to get acquainted and build a positive relationship with other students.

Is Each Student Accepted by Others in Your Classroom?

The first questions students of all ages ask as they enter a classroom rarely have to do with teachers or the academic curriculum. They ask: "Who is in my class?" "Who will I sit next to?" "What are their names?" "Will they like me?" Social acceptance dominates a child's thinking.

The need to belong is very important to a child's positive sense of self, yet many children go through school with few friends, and many are entirely without friends. Earlier, I shared with you the low percentages of students named as friends or potential friends by classmates. With the exception of tenth grade for girls and ninth grade for boys, where loyalty is strongest, as time goes by, fewer and fewer students are named as a friend by other students.

Friendship Skills for Students

Friends help young people feel affirmed in their worth.

You can't always be there to assist each student in his relationships with his peers and doing so isn't always your job, but you can help students develop the skills they need to make and sustain friendships. By creating better friendships, students feel more secure. Their own sense of worth is affirmed. This greatly contributes to their ability and willingness to be learners, and to their overall emotional well-being. Here is what you can do:

1. Help students to understand the nature of friendships. You can help your students to understand the nature of friendships and the value they place on them. When students understand more about developing friendships with their peers, they'll feel more confident about their ability to relate successfully to others, and be better able to change (or leave) the friendship. Furthermore, if they are the one who is abandoned, they are more likely to accept it without feeling unloved or unworthy. Books such as *Friendship Is Forever, Isn't It?* and *Unlocking Doors to Friendship* help students examine the nature of friendships and understand the influence friends have on each other. You can develop a special reading list for children and their parents. The suggested reading section at the back of this book list resources, and you can ask your librarian to construct a recommended reading list designed with the age of your students in mind.

2. Help students to develop an awareness of the cultural diversity of others. An awareness of the differences of others helps your students develop a greater tolerance for others, making them more capable of a broader range of friendships. Children need to learn that not everyone has the same interests, opinions, feelings, background, or capabilities as they do. Understanding this enables students to develop a healthy sense of self-regard for others.

3. Help students to develop an awareness of the capabilities and background of others. Show an appreciation for the diversity, talents, and aptitudes of others. Make a special effort to point them out. Read to students the stories of men and women of character, rich and poor, uneducated and educated. Teach by modeling a non-judgmental manner. Listen to what you have to say about others; prejudice is seldom "learned," but rather, an attitude that is passed on or instilled in others.

4. Encourage friendships in the classroom. Of the students in your classes, how many seem to be "friendless"? Ask yourself these questions:

■ Is there a child or two who appears to have a difficult time with a *particular* aspect of making friends? What specific social skills is she lacking? *Why is this child having this problem?* Maybe you notice she's always standing on the fringe of the group and is rarely included. Why is that? Is she shy about initiating a conversation? Does she make eye contact, does she smile, showing warmth and acceptance? Does she trust herself as a good friend?

■ What skills can I help my students develop so they will be liked and accepted by others in my classroom?

■ Does my teaching style encourage group activities and support students in understanding and appreciating others?

■ Do I encourage a cooperative learning environment?

5. Teach students skills for ending friendships. Just as your students need to know how to make and sustain friendships, they need to know how to end friendships. Techniques such as *role playing* teach students how to handle a particular situation, and help them evaluate the pros and cons of what to do in given situations. Best of all, this practice helps young people commit to the decision they have made. Here's an example of how role playing works at the high-school age level:

The Scenario:

Sixteen-year-old Julie has been asked by Ron to go to the school dance on Friday. However, she has decided she doesn't want to go out with him. Too embarrassed to call him up and tell him, she decides to stand him up — she just won't be home when he comes to pick her up. You want to convince her that's not appropriate, and teach her a better way to "undo" the date. You also want to increase her ability to confront Ron without backing down once she gets Ron on the phone or meets with him face-to-face. Here's how the role playing might take place:

Test Run No. 1:

Julie (*pretending to phone Ron*): "Hello, Ron?"
Teacher: "Hi, Julie!"
Julie: "I'm calling about the dance tomorrow night."
Teacher: "Oh, I know! I'm so excited about it! My dad said I could borrow his car instead of using my old beat-up one. Guess what, Julie, I'm taking us to dinner before the dance, and oh, I bought this really great new shirt and sweater in your favorite color! It's going to be so much fun. I'm so excited. I'll pick you up at 6:30."
Julie (*unprepared for Ron's enthusiasm and afraid to disappoint him*): "Oh, okay." (*She hangs up the phone, really disappointed in herself.*) "I don't care, I'm not going out with that nerd!" she yells. "Now I'm stuck with having to go out with him. I'll be so embarrassed. I'm not going to be seen with him. I'm going to the movies instead with Marsha!"

Test Run No. 2:

Julie: "Hello, Ron?"

Teacher: "Hi, Julie!"

Julie: "I'm calling about the dance tomorrow night."

Teacher: "Oh, Julie, I'm glad you called. I'm really sick. I won't be going to school tomorrow, and I won't be able to go to the dance. I'm really sorry. I hope I didn't ruin your weekend plans. Can we talk about it at school on Monday?"

Julie: "I'm sorry to hear you aren't feeling well, Ron. Yes, we can talk next week." *(Julie hangs up the phone, surprised, and pleased that she didn't call when she was angry with herself and take it out on him.)*

Test Run No. 3:

Julie: "Hello, Ron?"

Teacher: "Hello, Julie!"

Julie: "I'm calling about the dance tomorrow night. I know it's very late to back out, but I really have to. I hope you'll have time to make other plans."

Teacher: "Well, I'm sorry to hear that, Julie. I was really looking forward to going. Are you sure I can't change your mind?"

Julie: "Yes, I'm sure, Ron. I really must say no. I'm sorry."

Teacher *(sounding disappointed but accepting it)*: "OK. Bye, Julie. Oh, Julie, if you change your mind, please call me back. OK? Bye."

Other responses may occur, but the previous example illustrates how this kind of rehearsing can help a child build her confidence in handling potential situations. As Julie explained when the exercise was over, "Getting practice on how to handle the situation was really helpful to me because I really didn't know how to tell Ron that I had changed my mind about going out with him. To tell you the truth, before I role-played this, I was just going to not be home when he came to pick me up for the date. This exercise helped me see how standing him up would have made him feel awful and, as you said, rejected and humiliated. But I didn't think I had the nerve to call and cancel, even though there was no way I was going to go out with him. Role playing gave me the confidence to carry on the conversation I should have had in the first place."

The next phase of Julie's role playing would be for her to reverse roles with Ron, with Julie playing the part of Ron, and a male student playing Julie. This would help Julie build even more confidence in her ability to assert her decision. Such planning reduces the likelihood that she will be overwhelmed at the time of confrontation. Role-playing lets Julie test her ability to implement new behavior under stress. And just as importantly, by exchanging roles, she gets to put herself in the other person's place. These skills help students interact with others in a positive way and to understand the nature of friendships.

Utilizing Cooperative Learning in Your Classroom

Cooperative Learning is a model for teaching social skills within the core curriculum. It's a fluid, evolving process. When you enter a Cooperative Learning classroom, the first thing you notice are students clustered in small groups at workplaces around the room. As you watch, you notice an unusual level of concentration in the groups. Students focus on the assignment and materials, discussing their work, speaking one at a time, listening to and encouraging each other to share their thoughts and ideas. The teacher walks around the room, stopping to observe and offer guidance where needed. An atmosphere of support and friendliness pervades the entire room.

The groups of students might be discussing the best way to approach a problem or they may be studying spelling, history, or other subjects. In spite of the unusually high level of concentration, the students have the usual mix of skill levels and emotional development found in any classroom. This simple cooperation method works with any age or grade level, with any ability level, and with most curriculums. In this kind of an environment, students develop a sense of responsibility and dependability. They learn how to cooperate rather than compete and, as a result, they achieve greater success. There are three ways you can structure the tasks of learning: individualistic, competitive, and cooperative. Note the differences:

1. **Individualistic structure.** "I'm all alone in this." Each student is on his own and works alone to attain a specific goal. Each student's achievement is in no way related to any other student's achievement. For example, when working in a programmed-learning kit, a student moves from one level to another regardless of what any other student does.

2. **Competitive structure.** "It's me against you; someone wins and someone loses." Success is dependent upon the failure of others. Grading on a strict bell curve is an example of a competitive structure. Only 2% of the class population can earn "A's" regardless of how many points a student gets on the test. In a competitive environment, students have no incentive to help each other. In fact, quite the opposite occurs. The incentive is to "best" the others or to attempt to put others at a disadvantage, sometimes by withholding necessary information, or by giving wrong answers to other students in order to get ahead.

3. **Cooperative structure.** "We're in this together; we can only succeed if we do it together." In a cooperative group, students work together toward the completion of an assignment; they work together to achieve a common goal. Success is dependent upon all group members doing an equal share of the work and helping other group members learn the material. In fact, the group's study is not completed until each member of the group knows and understands the lesson content. This leads to a sense of group responsibility while developing group cohesion. This is not a situation where students are haphazardly grouped at tables, each doing the same or similar work, with permission to talk or socialize while completing assignments. The learning environment becomes cooperative

Cooperative Learning is a model for teaching social skills within the core curriculum.

only when students work together toward a common goal. The cooperative-structured classroom provides students the opportunity to develop leadership, self-confidence, self-esteem, and responsibility. Academic content is thus learned more efficiently.

Setting Up a Cooperative Learning Environment

The benefits of a cooperative learning environment are tremendous and merit attention. You will want to get formal training on creating this environment in your classroom, but here are the basics:

The first step is to set standards of expected behaviors for your students.

1. Set standards. The group development process begins with activities and techniques to establish a secure, supportive environment. The first step is to set standards of expected behaviors for your students. Students then have the opportunity to get to know you and each other through getting-acquainted activities. This helps students develop a high degree of trust and support for each other.

2. Assign group roles. Within this small group framework, students learn group roles. These roles help the group stay on track, give feedback, complete the group assignment, and measure achievement while teaching each member the skills needed to succeed in school and life. These skills include:

- getting your message across,
- attentive listening,
- giving and receiving praise and compliments,
- clarifying information,
- self-evaluation of skills and effort,
- developing responsibility and dependability,
- enhancing thinking skills, and
- increasing one's self-esteem and confidence level.

3. Teach thinking skills. Enhancing thinking skills is an inherent element in a cooperative lesson. As students share their thoughts and ideas, they provide each other with new ways to approach problems and complete tasks. Students learn there are other ways of viewing the world and meeting life's challenges. Cooperative Learning activities empower each student by providing the opportunity to develop the thinking skills necessary to function better in and out of school.

4. Reward task accomplishment with group grades. Each student may be given an individual grade or reward for each lesson and/or the group as a whole may be graded or rewarded for successfully working together. Group grades provide a clear and definite incentive. You also can use group bonus points or rewards as incentives to encourage students to cooperate with each other. In either case, students must receive a clear message that to succeed they must work together and that each group member must do his or her share of the work.

The core of the Cooperative Learning model is the teacher; you become a facilitator of learning rather than an "expert" who stands in front of the class disseminating facts and information. As a facilitator, you are a guide who provides direction and helps draw out the strengths of each student to accomplish the group objectives. Being a facilitator gives you the time to become more directly involved with your students.

While the concept of facilitating is fundamental to Cooperative Learning, it does not take the place of direct teaching. New information must always be taught. There are always times when the "teacher as expert" role is necessary. However, relying exclusively on this role robs students of the chance to think for themselves, to discover information, to make connections, and to share knowledge and ideas. By combining the traditional teaching role with facilitation, you vastly increase your effectiveness as a teacher as well as increase your students' abilities as learners.

As a facilitator, the teacher is a guide who provides direction.

You don't have to immediately change your whole teaching approach to realize the benefits of Cooperative Learning. In fact, if you are an elementary school teacher, choose a subject area that traditionally lends itself to group activities, such as science or social studies. For middle school and secondary teachers, begin with only one class period. As the process of Cooperative Learning becomes part of your regular classroom routine, learning will accelerate. There are three major reasons for the significant burst of academic achievement:

- First, a multi-modality approach to instruction takes place. Students are talking and listening to each other as well as reading and writing lesson materials.

- Second, the time that students are actively involved in learning is extremely high. Each student not only has a vested interest in completing the task, each also has a commitment to the group.

- Third, Cooperative Learning brings another crucial element into the learning process — enhancing thinking skills.

Strategies to Facilitate Positive Social Growth in Students

As an educator, you model behaviors that show tolerance for differences and the importance of acceptance of others. Your goal is to create a classroom that enables peer interaction to take place in a fun, friendly manner. Here are a few suggestions:

■ **Set up opportunities for interaction.** Allow students to work in small groups or pairs, rather than independently, to accomplish an assigned task. Assign homework activities that require communication and planning with classmates. Design lessons that provide hands-on experiences or field work that brings students closer to real situations that model and reinforce the importance of working together. This increases each student's opportunity to experience acceptance from others. Design lessons that allow students to shine in front of their peers. Additionally, design activities that encourage students to exchange ideas and feelings so classmates can share previously existing but unknown interests. Create lessons to improve students' abilities to empathize with others rather than to feel sorry for them because of their limitations. Highlight the strengths of classmates and discuss weaknesses positively as areas for improvement.

■ **Emphasize similarities.** Provide experiences that help students become aware of things they have in common. Activities requiring consensus enable common interests to surface. This not only encourages friendships, but assists students in understanding they are not totally different from their peers, and in reality, share more commonalities than differences. Students learn to recognize they are going through similar stages and self-identity problems. They build a sense of belonging within their peer groups.

■ **Avoid unhealthy competition.** While competition can be fun, too much competition alienates students and reduces the feeling of belonging. Work toward establishing a cooperative and cohesive classroom where students are encouraged to work toward the common good of all their classmates. Use peer feedback rather than teacher evaluation wherever possible.

■ **Provide students with opportunities to explore their feelings, attitudes, and actions toward others.** In doing so, students begin to break down the barriers that result from stereotypes. When young people involve themselves in community projects and participate in realistic situations, they become acquainted with unfamiliar situations.

■ **Provide opportunities for students to see the modeling of desirable social patterns.** Peer-modeling provides direction for helping socially isolated students. Many of these students exhibit antisocial behaviors, either consciously or subconsciously, that have become habits. By creating opportunities where students see their classmates act appropriately, they learn new behaviors. This helps them to clarify exactly what is expected for acceptance within their peer subculture.

Helping students develop people skills aids in forming friendships and, consequently, increases the student's sense of belonging, the fourth vital ingredient in building self-esteem.

Discussion

1. How much influence do you think teachers have over a student's friendships? How can you help a new or a shy child gain friends?

2. Should a teacher try to break up cliques? Are they healthy or unhealthy?

3. How can you help a "special" child, one who is handicapped or one who has an odd accent, fit in?

Chapter 11

COMPETENCE:
Helping Students Feel Capable

The fifth building block of self-esteem is competence — a sense of being capable. Being capable *empowers* students and actually contributes to how well they perform and achieve. This *attitude* of capability, more than IQ or opportunity, determines whether a student is willing and motivated to learn.

Feeling capable is the forerunner of *being* capable. Students who have an attitude of "I can do it!" are willing to go the extra mile. Because they do, they usually make it to the finish line. With an increased sense of confidence, the student expects to do well, and actually does better. In turn, positive experiences build the student's image of his competence. As the saying goes, "Success breeds success." Each success stimulates his efforts, and soon the student has a storehouse of positive reminders of his being capable. He feels like a winner!

Each success stimulates the student's efforts.

The 10 Characteristics of Highly Satisfied People

Seeing himself as a "can-do" person serves the student well in many ways. When he does poorly, he learns from it, then puts it behind him and moves on. Because he erases it from the error column, the outcome is a positive growth experience rather than a debilitating one. This attitudinal "skill" is central to doing well in life, as Gail Sheehy's findings reveal in her excellent book, *Pathfinders*. Sheehy wanted to know why, when met with crisis, some people were done in by the trauma, while others found creative ways to remove the obstacle or jump the hurdles, and continue on their way to achieve satisfying and nourishing lives. Sheehy's research reveals 10 characteristics of people with a high degree of life satisfaction. They were listed in this order:

1. My life has meaning and direction.
2. I have experienced one or more important transitions in my life, and have handled these in a positive way.
3. I rarely feel cheated or disappointed by life.
4. I have attained several long-term goals that are important to me.
5. Personal growth and development are important and ongoing for me.
6. I have mutually loving relationships in my life.
7. I have many friends.

8. I am a cheerful person.

9. I am not crushed by criticism.

10. I have no major fears.

Of those 10 qualities, one very important point stood out. *Highly satisfied adults said they rarely felt disappointed or cheated by life because they were able to learn from their experiences.* Nearly every one of these individuals had failed at something in a major way — but all had recast the experience in their minds. They had erased the outcome from the error column, and had come to see the experience as a plus. "What I learned from that experience . . ." was a common statement made by all. The so-called "bad experience" was found to be a useful one, so much so, that highly satisfied people rated it near the top of those events they said contributed to their success.

Exactly the opposite was the case with low self-esteem people, who described their crisis as a personal failure and a destructive experience, and saw themselves as victims. These individuals did not see themselves as capable of transforming the experience into one that would allow them to go forward with their lives. The experience had cast doubts on their capabilities, and they became fearful, cynical, and overwhelmed by their fate. Many were angry that life had dealt them such a fatal blow. Few saw how they themselves might have engineered their own fate, and even fewer took responsibility for what had happened. Unwilling to pick up the pieces and go forward, many low self-esteem people had actually dropped out of the workforce, abandoned their spouse or children, allowed their health to deteriorate, and coped through chemical or substance abuse.

How a Student's Attitude Affects His Performance

We know that a child's perception of his capabilities affects his actual performance. That doesn't mean that if the student has a good attitude he will do well in everything. It does mean he will approach his experiences with zest and zeal. For example, teachers say, "He's an eager learner," or "He's really motivated," or, "He'll do well because he expects to." This willingness to succeed or to attempt something new and difficult, even in unfamiliar terrain, means that he most likely will succeed. Confidence provides a mental attitude that prepares the child to respond according to his expectations. Look at the many positive characteristics of a child who feels capable:

A child's perception of his capabilities affects his actual performance.

Characteristics of a Child Who Feels Capable

- Is eager to try new things
- Is willing to try it again, to self-correct when he's met with failure
- Accepts challenges
- Uses mistakes as a learning tool

- Knows his strengths and leads with them
- Shares opinions and ideas freely
- Displays good sportsmanship
- Has effective coping strategies for handling defeat
- Recognizes accomplishments and achievements
- Gives himself positive self-statements and encouragement

Compare this to a student with a poor concept about his capabilities, and you'll see just the opposite. He magnifies his weaknesses and failures. A student with too few successes and frequent failures ends up with little incentive to try again. The attitude of "Why try? I'm just going to lose again anyway," becomes a self-defeating pattern. He believes his unsuccessful experience is a sign of personal failure and inadequacy. The message he gives himself is, "I won't be able to do it, I can't do it." Not feeling capable, he acts helpless. He depends on following others, even in areas where he is competent. He is unwilling to take risks, has an overriding fear of failure, and is a poor loser. He uses negative self-statements ("I'm so stupid") and discounts or discredits his achievement ("I was just lucky"). How can such traits possibly lead to feelings of accomplishment and satisfaction, and to experiencing outer achievement and success?

Help Each Student Decide He's a Winner!

You can help your students develop a greater sense of capability. The most obvious place to start is by examining your language. What are *you* saying? Is it positive and encouraging? Or not? Imagine that a student has just turned in his assignment. You check over the assignment and find it's sloppy, poorly written, and has several mistakes. What do you say? If you are not in a good mood when you speak to him, you might say:

"I thought you were trying to bring your grade up! Do you think this quality of work will do that? It's a mess. Look at it. I want you to start over again and don't bother turning it in again until you've done it right. You know better than this. You're just lazy! Look at Carol's paper, it's neat and her answers are correct. Why can't you be more like her?"

What message have you sent? First, you began with sarcasm. How would *you* feel if your principal walked into your room and said, "I thought you said you wrote the report? This is junk! Start over, and don't leave until you finish it." You would be discouraged and disheartened and probably would not want to redo the report.

Next comes the name-calling. You labeled the student lazy. That isn't a fair comment since he had, in fact, done the assignment. Besides, no one wants to be called names. When you call him lazy, you not only criticize the child, but unfairly make it sound as if he didn't even try. Perhaps worst of all, from the

A student with too few successes ends up with little incentive to try again.

viewpoint of a youngster, he was compared to other students and found wanting. Then you told him to start over again or not bother turning it in until he got it right. What a depressing thought! Starting over has the connotation that every-thing that has gone before is totally worthless and useless. What feelings is he left with? He has been attacked. He considers himself lazy, incompetent, and worthless. Do you think he will start over willingly?

Your comments, when negative, do little to build self-confidence and inspire renewed efforts. Remember, your goal is to increase his efforts and help him develop a sense of responsibility — *because* he feels capable. And, you want him to do the task willingly, because he sees himself as capable. Your language of encouragement is the first reason why he will do that.

Your goal is to increase the student's efforts and help him develop a sense of responsibility.

Compare this teacher's response to the previous example:

"Tyrone, I'm pleased that you have this assignment in on time. That shows effort and self-discipline, good qualities of yours. But there are sever-al things you must do in order to get a good grade on it. Look, this handwrit-ing is difficult to read and you've gone out of the margins. You seem to have gotten some food stains on this, too. Rewriting it neatly would improve this paper's appearance, and make it easier to read. Also, you might want to go over Chapter Six in the book. It'll really help you tighten up these answers. If you would like, I'll help you with those you're having trouble with. I remember how great your last extra credit assignment looked. Would you like me to help, or do you want to come back to me with it when you are done?"

What has this teacher done differently? This teacher has used the following steps to deliver effective criticism without eroding the student's self-esteem.

1. **Begin by praising effort.** Tell the student you appreciate his efforts. Everyone wants their efforts to be recognized and appreciated to feel that his effort is worthwhile. *Praise is the language of encourage-ment.* Mention his qualities as it relates to the task at hand. This rein-forces his sense of being capable, and he is *motivated* to redo the work rather than *forced* to redo it.

2. **Offer constructive criticism and guidance.** Use language that lets the student know what he needs to do to improve without making it a personal attack. Give the student concrete suggestions. The handwriting is hard to read, Chapter Six will give him answers, he can do something to change the situation.

3. **Critique the job, and not the student.** Tell him that the job was poorly done, not that he is a poor worker. He is not left feeling that *he* is bad, only that he didn't do a good enough job this time. His self-esteem is intact. In the previous example, you attacked the child personally, and

he was given no direction at all. Though he feels badly about *himself*, he hasn't learned much about shouldering the responsibility for properly completing his work.

Both effective and ineffective criticism may result in a paper being redone, but with effective criticism the student feels good about himself when he is finished, rather than feeling resentful. There's also a difference in the quality of the work. Here are some ground rules for developing "I am capable" language in your students.

Building Your Student's "I Am Capable" Language

■ **Build on the positive.** We are always correcting children's behavior. The goal is to do this in a way that is positive and constructive. Ask yourself, "How can I make my point, get the message across, and still leave my students feeling good about themselves? How can I phrase my comments so that each student knows I am telling her this because I want to help her, and because I know she can do better? How can I keep my students' self-esteem high while still changing the unwanted action?" Building on strengths is important because this is a time when the child most needs to be *encouraged*.

■ **Criticize the action, not the child.** Critique the activity, but don't demean the student in the process. Suppose an 11-year-old has been told to come straight back to the classroom after using the restroom. Ten minutes later he still hasn't returned, and you have to step out of class to find him. Instead of returning to class he has wandered over to the student center where he is watching students decorate for an assembly. By now he's missed his entire reading session. What could you do to criticize the action and not the child? What do you say?

> "Tommy, one of the rules that govern restroom breaks is that you are to come straight back to class afterward. Today, when you exceeded the three minutes that are allowed, I had to leave the rest of the class to go and look for you. You also missed out on your entire reading session and so now you will have to . . ."

Here the teacher informed Tommy of *why* and *how* the rule allows the teacher to be responsible about her student's safety. She makes it clear that the rules help *him*, not just teachers. You want to change the improper action, but leave him feeling that his safety and education are important to you. It would be useless to have your student hear, "You are an incredibly irresponsible person; I can't count on you to do anything right." As soon as your student hears the name-calling, he tunes you out. In addition, you defeated your own purpose by not making the connection in the student's mind between your criticism and his actions. The purpose here is not to vent your own irritation, but to help the student realize what he did was inappropriate so he won't repeat it in the future.

Effective criticism enables the student to feel good about himself rather than feeling resentful.

■ Call attention to good work and good behavior. When a student experiences success at one task, he is willing to move on to the next. Think of the little child who looks at a new tricycle and wonders if he'll ever be able to climb up that big thing and not fall off. With your encouragement and a number of unsuccessful attempts, he masters it. Before you know it, he is pedaling around the block and soon you can take off the training wheels. Once again, he doubts his abilities. You encourage him, and he surmounts the challenge. Many Band-Aids later, he's an expert. Soon, he's putting roadblocks in the way for a little challenge! "I am capable of doing this if I put my mind to it; I can accomplish whatever I set out to do," is an empowering message children send or *don't* send to themselves. Encouragement and positive reinforcement are effective ways of building capability and helping students *want* to achieve.

When a student experiences success at one task, he is willing to move on to the next.

Every Student Needs a Measure of Success

You also build competence by making sure that students have mastery in areas related to the new tasks to be learned. Grade levels in school are based on this concept. Courses are offered in sequence, increasing a child's skills in one area before progressing on to another, using test-proficiency as a way of making certain that a child has mastered one concept before introducing another. The child also moves from one grade to the next, a sign of accomplishment.

By tailoring the task to the child, and then gradually adding more responsibility, you build the student's sense of competence. When a child goes further and does something she wasn't certain she could do, she feels even more capable. Start out with tasks in which students have a strong chance for success. Let students do something that shows your confidence in them. They will progress beyond whatever bounds they had set in their own minds. Feeling more accomplished, they feel more worthwhile. You want the students' self-concept to include the idea that they are responsible persons, capable of being depended upon. Praise is the language of encouraging responsibility in children, so that they'll be encouraged to try and try again.

We all need to feel successful in our work, and students are no exception. But in order for a child to succeed, he must first believe he can. The lower his self-esteem, the less willing he is to try again. The more positive statements he hears from you, the more he tries, and the better he does. He needs positive feedback and praise in order to be encouraged. Teachers utilize this concept when they give gold stars to praise good work at school. All students need and deserve a chance to have gold stars and happy faces decorate their papers, regardless of what grade they are in.

Is each child getting all the gold stars he needs from you? Here are some ground rules for giving gold stars:

Ground Rules for Giving Praise

■ **Effective praise is personal and individual.** It need not be heard by the entire class. Be sincere and share it heart-to-heart with the individual student. Of course, this is not to imply that you shouldn't compliment a student in front of the entire class.

■ **Praise must be immediate.** The best time to give praise is right when it is deserved. The longer you delay your praise, the less effective it is.

■ **The praise must be deserved.** Be sure that the praise you give is deserved, or you lose credibility with the student. Students know whether they really have earned praise.

■ **Praise must be behavior-centered.** Praise specific behaviors and not just positive attributes. Stick to what the student did. Telling a poor student that he is an A student doesn't fit his inner self-image and, consequently, the praise will be met with disbelief and discounted. In developing achievement, it's important to relate the praise to a particular behavior.

■ **Be specific.** The most effective praise is concrete and tells the student exactly what was done well. When you see good behavior, don't say "great," but rather, "Jerome, you did a nice job on spelling the words correctly in those 10 sentences." Specific praise lets the student know *what* he did well and, as a result, *he's more likely to repeat the behavior.*

■ **Use praise consistently.** All students need praise, especially low self-esteem children. Giving praise one or two times is not enough for students with low self-esteem. Their internal image is so ingrained that you need to repeat the praise for similar behaviors two to three times before the message is internalized and accepted. Don't feel you're becoming a broken record; praise frequently for the same observed behavior. Younger students and low self-esteem students tend to forget their praiseworthy moments.

■ **Use awards and rewards.** Praise can be more than words; it can include awards and rewards. These are different from bribes. Bribes do not enhance self-esteem. A reward, on the other hand, especially if it's unexpected and spontaneous, shows the student he did something special and that he deserves something special. It puts him in the spotlight for a moment, and *lets him feel his accomplishment.*

■ **Avoid backhanded praise.** A backhanded compliment mixes praise with insult. It gives the student praise for what she did well, but at the same time, reminds her of earlier failure. No wonder students don't feel good when they receive it. For example, compare these statements:

> **Backhanded Praise:** "That's pretty good, considering how you waited to the last minute to do it!"

> **Real Praise:** "You did a very good job on this report, Marianne."

> **Backhanded Praise:** "It's about time you handed it in."

> **Real Praise:** "I'm glad you got it done."

Be sure praise is deserved, or you will lose credibility.

Helping Students Learn from Mistakes

Failure is an opportunity to begin again.

Henry Ford was right when he said, "Failure is the only opportunity to more intelligently begin again." I see so many young people who have experienced so little success that they're afraid of making even more mistakes. These students won't initiate friendships that appear too difficult to strive for, they don't go out for activities if they think they won't do well, nor will they take a course in school they think will be too difficult. Many schools have a rich curriculum with excellent courses designed to teach exciting skills, but unless these courses are mandated, many young people won't sign up for them. And because so many parents distance themselves from the schools and don't realize how rich the school's curriculum really is, they are unable to counsel their children about courses that might help them become more capable.

I often share the Thomas Edison story of success versus failure with young people to help them keep trying after they've made a mistake. Edison didn't create the electric light on the first try. He didn't wake up one day and say, "Today's goal is to create the electric light!" Edison failed, and failed, and failed.

Finally an associate of his said, "Edison, you should give up. You've failed thousands of times."

"No, I haven't failed thousands of times," Edison replied. "On the contrary, I have successfully eliminated thousands of ideas that do not work!"

This analogy applies to helping students build their sense of competence. Be encouraging. When teachers write specific comments of encouragement on a test or assignment where a child didn't do well, the student strives to improve performance. When students do not receive positive and helpful comments, they fail to improve on future assignments. This is true for both good and poor students. By receiving feedback in the form of constructive encouragement, young people know specifically what to do in order to improve, but as importantly, they *want* to do better. And though you offer praise for your student's achievements, a child must see the value of her own work, too. Teach her to acknowledge herself in the process.

Emotional Self-Management Skills

Being capable is more than academic achievement and success. Young people also obtain a sense of how capable they are by being in charge of their emotional lives — specifically, being able to control or change one's thought process, reframing it in a positive way. This is especially important because children often think that parents, teachers, or friends cause them to react the way they do. In their minds, *someone else* is responsible.

1. Controlling inner thoughts. You can help your students feel in charge of their emotions. Teach the concept that thoughts determine behaviors. Help students see it's not so much the event that determines their behavior, as how they think about it. For example, you're driving along, and begin to think about an unpleasant confrontation you had with someone a day, week, or month earlier. Soon you find yourself clenching the wheel tightly and driving faster. Recalling the situation has made you upset all over again, yet you're alone in the car! Recalling the incident produces the same emotions as if it had just happened. But, you get to be in charge of your feelings, and consequently, behavior outcomes.

As you've no doubt experienced, many students *feel, act,* and then *think,* when they would be better served to *think, feel,* and then *act.* Perhaps you have heard someone say, "I can't help what I do, it just happens." This assumes that thoughts and feelings occur independently and are not under our control. However, the opposite is true. Rarely does a feeling "just happen." There is a direct connection between thoughts, feelings, and behaviors. Let's look at this in operation:

Thoughts determine behavior.

Mr. Hanson told Robbie that he couldn't barge in line on the playground. "I know you're anxious to play on the slide, Robbie," Mr. Hanson said, "but you must wait your turn in line like everyone else." Robbie begins to process this message. Here are two possible scenarios of Robbie's thinking:

> **Robbie's thoughts:** "Mr. Hanson is mad at me. He knows how much I want to play on the slide. If he liked me, he wouldn't embarrass me in front of the other kids."
>
> **Robbie's feelings:** Upset, angry, defensive.
>
> **Robbie's behavior:** He stomps off to play on the swings, shouting how unfair his teacher is.

Robbie assumes that it is his teacher who made him upset and angry, and therefore, he has a right to be defensive. After all, the teacher reprimanded him. In this case, what Robbie is thinking is irrational and it affects his behavior in a negative way. A different and more positive scenario on Robbie's part might be as follows.

> **Robbie's thoughts:** "I wish I had stayed in line. I know the rule, and it doesn't feel good to be reminded of it in front of the other students."
>
> **Robbie's feelings:** Rational, feeling responsible.
>
> **Robbie's behavior:** Speaking to Mr. Hanson he says, "I'm sorry. I know I'm supposed to wait in line. If I apologize for shoving Timmy and get at the back of the line, can I still play on the slide?"

Helping students learn the connection between thinking and behavior can have high payoffs! The student learns that he is capable of being responsible for his actions. Now, he needs to know how to change unwanted thoughts.

2. Changing unwanted thoughts. Dean receives a low grade on his first math test. He tells himself he is dumb and not capable of doing the work. He believes failing this one math test means he will fail all his others. So, he skips math class on the day of his next test. Dean's coping style was affected negatively by what he has told himself about his abilities. Beliefs that work against him put limits on what he attempts. Each student must be able to distinguish between the situation itself and what he says to himself about it. It doesn't make sense that Dean should skip math class simply because he failed one exam. Unwanted or irrational thoughts can be changed to positive ones by using a process called "thought-stopping."

Once the student is aware of how his inner thought works for or against his ability to achieve and excel, he can learn to change the negative thoughts. When a student tells himself limiting statements, he should visualize a "stop sign." This mental stop sign is a signal to stop thinking dysfunctional thoughts. Dean told himself because he failed a math test, he would fail again. He skipped class to avoid repeating an unpleasant situation. If Dean used thought-stopping, then he could have replaced the negative thought with a positive one, such as:

Once a student is aware how his inner thoughts affect him, he can learn to change those that limit him.

- "Just because I failed one test doesn't mean I'll fail all other math tests."
- "Failing a test doesn't have to mean I'm dumb."
- "I should study harder next time."
- "I could attend review sessions and ask for extra help if I feel I need it."

Help students learn how to reshape negative messages by focusing on the things that they do well. The goal is to get students to think about the *approach* they bring to schoolwork, relationships, and life.

3. Rescripting negative messages. Another way you can get students to turn negative thoughts into positive ones is by having them write a sentence on something they don't like about themselves, and then rewrite the sentence, this time using a positive rather than a negative statement.

Example: School is hard for me.

Rewrite: I enjoy all my subjects except algebra. I did well in math class, but I don't yet understand all the concepts of algebra. I need more help in that class.

Example: I am unpopular.

Rewrite: I'd like to be friends with Karen and Debra, but I'm not certain they want my friendship.

If a student thinks he's not a good student, he may find school difficult, and this contributes to his not liking school. Likewise, if he seeks someone's friendship but doesn't get it, he may feel unpopular. Changing, rewriting, or rescripting the way he thinks about himself develops competence because when he sends more positive messages to himself, he is more likely to have the courage to go forward when things get tough. When the child does well, he starts that wonderfully contagious success cycle that contributes to his excelling in his day-to-day work, and in his relationships with you and others.

Problem-Solving Skills

Too often, students feel powerless and become victimized by others. An important part of self-esteem is feeling able to cope with the everyday challenges, including managing one's emotions.

You can help students learn and acquire skills that will change helpless feelings to "can-do" ones. Taking responsibility and gradually exerting more influence over his own actions helps the student feel capable. Students who previously floundered when faced with a dilemma now find they have resources to take charge. They make decisions and choose what the outcome will be. A good place to start is to help students learn how to solve problems, generate alternatives, and evaluate the consequences.

Having a problem and not knowing how to remedy it can be as debilitating as it is frustrating. But finding a solution and getting out of a dilemma is made even more difficult when young people aren't sure what the problem is, only that one exists. In groping for a solution, they may act impulsively or make rash decisions. Effective problem-solving is a four-step process that involves identifying the real problem; searching for sound solutions and recognizing the consequences; trying them out; then evaluating the outcome. This approach works with secondary, middle-school, and elementary-age children. I've included two examples.

Having a problem and not knowing how to remedy it can be as debilitating as it is frustrating.

This process begins by asking four simple questions:

1. **What is the problem?**
2. **How can I solve it, what are the consequences?**
3. **What is my plan?**
4. **How did I do?**

Fifteen-year-old Mia has invited Jessica to go skiing with her and her parents in two weeks. Jessica, also 15, has told her parents of the plans and has asked for permission to go. They say that she can, based on good grades on the next report card, due out in two weeks. Jessica tells Mia "yes" and her parents arrange for her to accompany them on the trip. The report card comes out the day prior to the planned ski trip. Jessica received two failing grades. She is certain her parents will not let her go on the trip now, so she doesn't give them the report card. Using this four-step procedure can result in an effective problem resolution. Let's apply it.

1. What is the problem?

Jessica has accepted an invitation to a ski trip, and has permission based on specific criteria; Mia and her parents expect her to go on the trip with them and have made special arrangements. Jessica does not want to break the trust with her parents by not revealing the report card, but she wants Mia to accept her. After all, Mia is the most popular girl in school and besides, Jessica has told all her friends that she is going.

2. How can I solve it, what are the consequences?

Action: Jessica could go along without telling her parents of the grades and by not revealing the report card until after she returns home from the ski trip.
Consequence: She will break the trust she and her parents have established.

Action: She could ask her parents for permission to go based on the promise to work harder and get better grades the next quarter.
Consequence: Could be risky, her parents might say no.

Action: She could call Mia and tell her that she has decided she doesn't want to go on the trip.
Consequence: Mia will feel offended, and the friendship will be strained.

(Have students generate as many other alternatives as possible.)

3. What is the plan? (Have students decide what course of action Jessica will take.) Help students examine the outcome of proposed actions by asking a question such as, "If you do that, what would happen?" This question is often followed by, "And then what would happen?" Ask students to generate as many alternatives to the problem as they can, then help them assess the potential impact of each option. Your goal is to help students learn how a different alternative leads to a different outcome.

4. How did I do? Have students decide what is the likely outcome, and how she will feel about herself as a result. Here is an example of this process used with the elementary age student:

1. What is the problem?
Danny called me "stupid" and it made me mad!

2. How can I solve it?

Action: I could call him stupid back.
Consequence: He will stay angry.

Action: I could punch him.
Consequence: He might hit me back.

Action: I could tell him how angry it makes me.
Consequence: He would understand my feelings.

> Your goal is to help students learn how a different alternative leads to a different outcome.

Action: I could ignore it.

Consequence: He might continue to call me names.

3. **What is my plan?** Ask the student, "When will you do this?"

Plan: I'm going to tell him to stop name-calling. **When:** I'll tell him on the bus tomorrow morning.

4. **How did I do?**

My plan worked great. I said it politely. I didn't get in a fight. Danny said he was sorry.

When a youngster feels he is good at some things, he's willing to learn how to do other things. Aware of his strengths, he accepts the areas where he's less competent, and can do so without developing victim-behavior. He participates in class. He feels secure in sharing his opinions and ideas. Because he feels capable, he is willing to try rather than give up at the first sign of difficulty. Because he tries, he experiences successes that encourage him to try new things. He is self-empowered through realistic and achievable goals, and therefore, he has initiative.

> **He is willing to try rather than give up at the first sign of difficulty.**

Discussion

1. A child who considers himself capable of learning puts in the effort to study, and attempts to overcome frustrations when something doesn't come easily. A child with low self-esteem is defeated before he begins. He assumes that he's not intelligent enough to master the material, and gives up at the first obstacle. Give an example of how you've seen this played out in your teaching experience.

2. A child without goals has a difficult time relating school success to the outside world. He also has difficulty relating to others in school, and doesn't develop the friendships — the support system — that makes school a fun and endurable place. In your experiences as an educator, how have you seen this played out?

3. How can you be supportive of your colleagues in a way that contributes collectively to synergy, team spirit, an exciting work environment. How can you support each other in the tough job of teaching?

4. What do you do to create a sense of personal competence for youth in *your* classroom?

5. How does the *school* environment provide for student competence? What else needs to be done?

Chapter 12

COMPETENCE:
Helping Parents Understand Their Child's World of Work

There are many payoffs in school for high self-esteem children. For example, a high self-esteem child is willing to stand up for what he considers his right. Recently, I saw proof of this when my daughter's friend, Debra, received a B- on a paper she turned in for her History class. Debra felt she deserved a better grade and presented her case to the teacher. The teacher took the time to sit down with her and explain in detail exactly where he thought the paper was weak. He also listened closely to her argument. The result was that Debra received a B, a slightly higher grade. Even more important, she received extra attention from the teacher and felt good knowing that she had the courage to stand up for what she believed she had earned. You can bet that because she has presented herself in that way to her teacher, she will win the teacher's respect, consideration, and attention on future assignments. That additional attention will increase her desire to achieve, and it will result in another measure of success, adding even more to her positive sense of self.

It's doubtful that a child with low self-esteem would take on this challenge. She would shrug and say, "I got this grade because the teacher doesn't like me." She would feel powerless to bring about any other outcome. With each downbeat experience, she becomes less willing to stand her ground.

Why High Self-Esteem Children Do Better in School

Notice the behavior cycles created here. A child with strong self-esteem performs actions that allow her self-esteem to be *strengthened* even more. A child with low self-esteem doesn't perform such actions, and as a result, her self-esteem is *lowered* even more.

A student's ability to manage his everyday world gives him a sense of competence. Since children spend a large portion of their waking hours in school — approximately 15,000 hours in an educational system from kindergarten through twelfth grade — you can imagine why a sense of feeling competent in the school environment is important. At the end of his formal school "career," the student will be a 12- or 13-year veteran of a mandated educational experience. Is it any

A student's ability to manage his everyday world gives him a sense of competence.

wonder that his feelings of competence are influenced by his performance in a place where he spends so much time?

Certainly educators influence a child's sense of performance, but parents do, too. In fact, when parents don't participate, the educator's job is more difficult, and sometimes impossible, to do.

The Child's Workplace

I have always been amazed at how little parents know about the real nature of their child's school experiences. Some parents are surprised to find out that school closely resembles the fast-paced and pressured environment of a business organization. The demands on the child-as-student in school, and the demands on the adult in the work setting are quite similar. We should help parents think of school life in ways they can understand. Being a student is their child's *occupation*, learning is his *role*, education is his *career*, and school is his *organization*. School is his workplace.

> **Being a student is a child's occupation, learning his role.**

For many students, school is an intense and frustrating experience. Indeed, some students don't endure as well. Some drop out psychologically, and others drop out physically. No one wants this to happen, but sometimes it seems that parents don't help their children with school.

Unfortunately, parents don't receive a school "career manual" similar to the job manuals that companies issue to employees to explain company policies and ways to maneuver successfully through the maze of organizational life. While a school often provides a brochure on the district's discipline policy, this mostly spells out the procedures for taking action against the student when he has violated the rules. Both parents and students need more information.

Parents Make the Difference

"The difference between a good school and a great school is parent involvement," says Bessie McLemore, principal of Fulton High School in Atlanta, Georgia, and 1987 National PTA Hearst Educator-of-the-Year. "It sounds simple but it's true," she says. "Parents can improve their child's ability to learn and achieve in school by helping their child at home, by showing their child that they value education, and by keeping a close watch on their child's schooling. Parents can improve their child's school just by playing an active role in its various programs and functions."

In a book called *Talks to Parents: How to Get the Best Education for Your Child*, the National PTA lists the 10 things that teachers wish parents would do.

10 Things Teachers Wish Parents Would Do

1. Be involved. Parent involvement correlates to student learning and school improvement.

2. Provide resources at home for learning. Parents should have books and magazines available and they should read with their children on a weekly basis.

3. Set a good example. Parents should show their children that they believe that reading is both enjoyable and useful. Parents who spend all their time in front of the TV don't accomplish this.

4. Encourage their children to do their best in school. Parents need to show their children that they believe education is important and that they want their children to do their best.

5. Emphasize learning. Too many parents get caught up in *only* supporting their child's athletics, and in preparing their children for college. Support *learning*, too.

6. Support school rules and goals. Parents should take care not to undermine school rules, discipline, or goals.

7. Use pressure positively. Parents should encourage children to do their best, but should not pressure children by setting goals too high or by scheduling too many activities.

8. Call teachers early if there is a problem. Problems take time to solve. Don't wait for teachers to call with the bad news.

9. Accept their responsibility as parents. Don't expect the school and teachers to take over all the obligations of parents. Parents should teach children basic discipline at home rather than leaving this to teachers.

10. View drinking and excessive partying as a serious matter. This takes a toll on classroom performance. While parents are concerned about drug abuse, many fail to recognize that alcohol is the drug most frequently abused by youngsters. Children can't learn in an altered state.

Parents would be surprised to find that they don't have to invest a great deal of time to significantly influence their child's school success. Half an hour a day of reading and talking to their child, discussing their child's homework, upcoming exams, and other work, makes a big difference. A few hours a month volunteering at their child's school, attending PTA meetings and supporting the PTA's efforts shows children their parents consider the schoolplace important and purposeful. By showing their child that education is important, the child will become a better student. That's why I've written this section addressed to parents. Please share it with them. The bottom line is that parents are extremely important to a student's sense of competence in his school performance and achievement.

16 Things to Ask Parents to Do

When parents help their children develop skills in managing their "world of work," their children's self-esteem is strengthened, rather than debilitated. Here are 16 things to ask parents to do to help their children be competent in their workplace.

1. Help your child get organized. Your child will need the appropriate "tools" to work. Every child needs a quiet study area, safe from interruption, and equipped with a good light. He needs a desk and a bookcase. Shop for pencils,

Not having a place to work is a reason why many children don't want to do homework.

paper, and other supplies he needs in his role as a student. Set up a filing system and show him how to use it. Get a large month-at-a-glance wall calendar to record work assignments and school-related activities. This makes it easy for a child to plan particular projects and assignments, as well as schedule social activities. It also makes him feel like a "professional" doing a job. This should be *his* work space and, if possible, not a shared space. It doesn't have to be a large area, just a space that he associates with doing homework. Not having a place to work, or the tools to do it, is a big reason why many children don't want to do their homework.

2. Set parameters for study time. During study time, there should be no TV or stereo Walkman, and no phone calls. Phone calls can be made after homework projects are done, or between studying different subjects as a way to take a break. If your child needs to clarify an assignment by talking to a fellow student, two to three minutes is sufficient. If your child is in high school and has unrestricted phone privileges, discourage lengthy phone calls *during* study time. You want to teach your child the power of uninterrupted concentration. Explain to him why this is a good practice.

3. Agree on a regular time for studying. Whether you decide this time is immediately after school or after the evening meal, be as consistent as possible. A routine helps your child to do his homework consistently, day after day, and eliminates many excuses for not having the time to do it.

4. Help your child to identify his work style. Your child may be able to complete all her studying and homework in a single session, or she may do better if she studies for 20 minutes, takes a break, and then comes back to it. Each child is different. The important thing is that she recognizes her own style for producing her best work. You can help your child identify her work style by discussing how you prepare for productive work. If she's overly tired, or unwilling to do a particular assignment, how can she prepare for productive work? Perhaps she can put on a good tape, or take a brisk walk or a 10-minute bike ride. Help her learn to renew her energy and channel it. If you know she is simply too tired, don't force it. She won't be productive if she's unable to summon the energy.

5. Show an active interest in your child's schoolwork. This sends the message that you care about your child's school career, and that he should, too. You convey the message that school is purposeful and that learning is important. You can show your interest by asking *meaningful* questions. If you ask, "What did you do in school today?" and your child answers, "Nothing," ask more specific questions based on what you know is being taught. Rather than asking, "How was your day?" ask about what he is learning. Does he feel he is showing improvement? What contributed to the good grades as well as to the poor ones? What is his favorite subject and why? Is the "A" a mark of achievement or was the work too easy? Was the "D" because he doesn't understand the material, or was it because the finals were taken the day after the three-day band trip out of the city and he wasn't prepared? Ask these questions, even though you may feel you know the answers. Become familiar with your child's courses, and know what's being taught and what's expected. What books will be read? How much homework will be required? What major long-term projects can be anticipated? Is your child likely to need help with any projects? Remember, school is tough for "A" children, too. Your attitude is all-important. Children do as their parents do, not as they say. If you are enthusiastic about new books and new ideas, your child will be enthusiastic, too. A half an hour a day spent reading and talking to your child makes a big difference. When you show your children that their education is important to you, you influence how they do in school.

Parents should convey the message that learning is important.

6. **Determine what on-the-job skills your child needs.** Use clues from report cards, teacher conferences, and aptitude tests to become familiar with your child's strengths and weaknesses so you'll know where you can help. Is he lacking a particular skill? Can you obtain special tutoring for a problem area? Is there a physical problem, perhaps with eyesight or hearing? Is there a learning disability?

7. **Ask about his "co-workers."** Who are his friends at school and why? How much time do they get to be together in favorite school activities? Do they eat lunch together? Who are good students and why? Who are not such good students and why? Has he noticed that he's a better learner when he feels like a friend, and a better friend when he's feeling successful in school? What are his thoughts about this realization?

8. **Talk to your child about his teachers.** Think about the teachers you had in school — the ones you liked and those you didn't. How did they make you want to learn? Were some teachers so exciting that you looked forward to their classes? Did some teachers talk with students rather than lecture to them day after day? Did you notice that in some classes time flew by while in others you were often daydreaming and waiting for the class to be over? Does your child like his teachers? Why or why not? What teacher(s) does your child find exciting, and why? In most cases, children choose a career based on a *special* teacher. Who is this *special* teacher for your child?

9. **Teach time management skills.** For most children, whether in elementary, junior high or high school, there never seems to be enough time outside of school to cope with assignments, friends, extracurricular activities, and family. Often it seems to the child there is no time left over for herself. Even during the school day, one of the greatest pressures on your youngster is time. An important step in helping her learn to manage her time is to set up a daily or weekly "to-do" list. It should not be long and detailed, but should contain those things that she wants to accomplish each day or week. Priority-setting is also important. Help your child to generate the list, and then delineate the one or two tasks that are the most urgent. Set a timetable and estimate the length of time necessary to perform each task. Break long-term projects down into manageable parts so she can begin

on them, and not wait until the last minute to do something. Variations on the planning form shown below works for most students from second grade up.

One of the greatest pressures on children is time.

DAILY PLANNING SHEET	
Today's date:	
Subject area:	
Assignment:	
When due:	
Don't forget to:	

10. Help your child with homework. When children become students, parents often become "students," too. Helping your child can be a frustrating and tension-filled experience for both parent and child. Not all parents can help their children with homework. If you find you are unable to help your child — for whatever reason — find an outside source. Children enjoy working with others, and this can alleviate the tension and additional constraints on parental time. Older teenagers and college students often enjoy working with younger children. When you help your child with homework, here are some things to keep in mind:

- Have patience. Allow your child to learn at his own pace.
- Encourage your child to do his best work, but recognize that this work may not necessarily be "A" level.
- Let your child know you are proud of him for doing his best.
- Allow him time to relax between difficult or long assignments.
- Praise positive efforts as well as work achievements.
- Don't name-call when he's having a rough time grasping a concept.
- Don't *you* get discouraged.

11. Tutor your child. Aside from daily assignments, there may be an area where your child needs special help in acquiring a skill. Tutoring your own child is often a difficult undertaking. Not many parents or children have enjoyed one another in these roles. Remember, the important thing is to enhance your child's sense of capability while preserving the relationship between the two of you. When you're ready to help, this approach works best. For example, you can say, "Michael, I talked to your Math teacher this morning. She told me you were doing well with simple equations, but that you were having some problems with graphing. I can help you with that. How does that sound to you?" This opens up lines of communication. Remember that you *want him to want* the extra help. You want his participation and commitment to do better. Without it, you may be the only one working for improvement. Here are some special considerations to keep in mind when tutoring:

■ **Sit next to your child rather than across from him.** It's easier for both of you to see the lessons, and it encourages a friendlier relationship.

■ **If you find that the tutoring session is unpleasant for you or your child, don't get discouraged.** Be patient and ask your child for his explanation. His reaction may be based on the fear of not being able to do the work, yet he may not want you to know it for fear you'll be disappointed.

■ **Be sure that the directions you give are presented slowly and clearly.** For some children the major difficulty is not in mastering the subject matter, but in following directions.

■ **Work through one step at a time.** This keeps your child's attention on the work and gives you a closer look at where the difficulties lie. For example, if you are doing addition problems, present them one at a time rather than asking your child to do a page of 15 or 20 problems all at once.

■ **When your child speaks to you, or when you are speaking to him, be sure to look at him.** Sometimes it's easier to see confusion and frustration than it is to hear it.

■ **Don't skip any problems.** Wait for an answer to each one. This helps your child develop the habit of working on difficult items rather than passing them by.

■ **Minimize your use of phrases such as, "That's wrong."** Instead, respond to a wrong answer by restating the question and supplying your child with more clues to help him determine the correct answer. After he gets the correct answer, it's useful to go over the questions in its original form without the clues, but with praise.

Without a child's participation, you may be the only one working for improvement.

12. Make homework fun! There is no need to be too serious. It's much more enjoyable to work together when you can gently tease each other, or make silly puns. Personalize the lessons with humor. Parents of small children know how much they enjoy it when the parent is wrong: "You mean 'KAT' is not how to spell cat?" a parent might ask. You can carry it over into any subject. Mnemonics, or memory devices, can become works of art between parent and child. I still remember my Uncle Ray teaching me the divisions in biology: Kingdom - Phylum - Class - Order - Family - Genus - Species with "Kinky People Come Over for Great Sex!" Twenty-five years later, I can still rattle them off!

13. Follow your child's progress. Your child's performance appraisals or report cards tell you how he's doing. Remember that bad grades don't automatically appear. If you've been watching weekly reports, and grades on papers and tests, you should have some idea of how your child is doing. Even if your children's report card isn't as good as you would like it to be, look for something positive — a grade raised in Math, or a teacher's comments about how hard your child is working — and show your child you're pleased with his success, even though you're concerned with his less successful efforts. If you ground your child because of a bad report card, or if you yell and scream and tell him he is lazy or stupid, you're not doing anything to improve his grades; in fact, you're probably making the situation worse. Be proactive. Start by doing something you can make a difference in, now.

14. Meet your child's "boss." Meet your child's teacher at the beginning of the term. Many parents feel uncomfortable about contacting their child's teacher, and even more anxious if the teacher calls to request a meeting. Such feelings may be related to the fact that the teacher is still associated with the parents' own childhood, when the teacher may have been a strong authority figure who defined what was right or wrong, who passed judgment, or who was overly critical. Keep in mind that most teachers are parents, too. They often come to parent-teacher conferences with their own apprehensions and uncertainties about how they will be viewed by *you*. Understanding the perspective of the teacher, as well as your own feelings, will help to make your relationship with the teacher productive and enjoyable.

15. Schedule a "business meeting" with the teacher. Some parents believe that parent-teacher conferences occur for one of two reasons: their child is behaving badly, or their child is having serious problems keeping up with schoolwork. Conferences are held for these reasons, but they're not the only conditions why conferences occur. A parent-teacher conference can be scheduled to report on the child's progress; to compare the teacher's understanding of the child with that of the parents' when the teacher has noticed something in the child's behavior that could be of concern; and to ask parents for specific help with a problem, for example, if a child is having difficulties with schoolwork that may be related to the home environment. Teachers aren't the only ones who can schedule conferences. You can take the initiative, too. If you have specific questions, or if you want to know how your child is doing, or if you think there's a problem, make an appointment with the teacher immediately. Call the school to set it up. Don't expect to get a teacher out of class to speak to you, but do expect that the teacher will return your call. If you don't hear from the teacher within two days, call again. If, after your second call, there is no return call, ask to speak with the assistant principal. If you speak a language different from that of the teacher, ask if the school will provide an interpreter.

Children experience job burnout just as adults do.

16. Watch out for the "overinvolvement syndrome." Children experience job burnout just as adults do. Burnout may be due to an after-school job that takes up too many hours, or it may be caused by too many social activities, or too much time spent with friends, on dates, or on other activities. Is your child trying to do too much at once? Discuss with your child which activities can be cut back. Your child will be relieved that you have intervened.

Children whose parents are actively involved in their education often score higher on achievement tests than do students who have more ability or greater social and cultural advantages but whose parents are not involved. The U.S. Department of Education confirmed: "What parents do to help their children learn is more important to academic success than how well-off the family is."

These and other similar reports give testimony to how important parents are in developing a student's competence in school. Says Ann Lynch, 1989-91 National PTA president, "Whether you are a middle-class suburbanite, a minority parent living in the slums of a major city, or a resident of a rural area, whether you are a doctor or a dishwasher, your involvement will mean that your child will learn more and do better in school."

Discussion

1. Is it valid to say a child's school is her work? What similarities and differences exist?

2. How does parental involvement lead to enhanced self-esteem for students? Can the added pressure backfire?

3. How can teachers involve "problem parents," those with little time, or education, or motivation?

Exercise

1. Have students write an essay on the 16 things that parents should do and what they think their parents are doing. Share the essays with parents.

2. Have parents come to school for career day, or give presentations on one of their typical work days.

3. Design a Parents' Progress Report, a log where parents can track their parent-teacher conferences, calls, notes, and general involvement.

Chapter 13

MISSION:
Helping Students Develop a Sense of Purpose

Having a sense of mission or purpose is the sixth building block that helps students gain a positive self-esteem. Feeling purposeful gives you the inner knowledge that your life has meaning and is worthwhile. Students with a sense of purpose develop inner well-being because they have in mind specific aims or intentions of what they want to do and become. Because they have a vision, they have direction. This is not to say that an 8-year-old student knows that she wants to be a gardener or an engineer, but she does know whether she is drawn to music, people, or animals. Each time the student focuses on what provides meaning for her, she's energized in the process. Inner peace, appreciation, and greater self-knowledge are the result.

Students who have discovered things that are important to them are more vibrant and optimistic. They have a zest for living and will do what's necessary to realize their needs and goals. Because what's going on in their own lives seems exciting, they are more self-motivated and self-directed.

A student who feels purposeful is quite different than a student who doesn't believe his life has meaning. Unable to feel fulfilled, the low self-esteem student is listless, aimless, and often turns to others for self-fulfillment. This may lead to hanging out with a bad crowd or joining a gang. The low self-esteem student tends to blame others for his plight and is not accountable for his actions. I've worked with both young children and older youth who have resigned themselves to feeling powerless about their lives. They have opted to be victims, not even attempting to participate in their lives in an active and vital way. Helping students find purpose and meaning is a critical element of vibrant health, motivation, ambition, learning, achievement, self-respect, and well-being.

Students with a sense of purpose develop inner well-being.

Feeling Purposeful Improves Success in School

Feeling purposeful enhances self-esteem and raises the level of a student's performance in school. The Coleman Report, a comprehensive investigation of American education, concluded that the degree to which a student felt his life had meaning and direction was the second most significant determinant (parent support was the first) of whether he met with failure or success in his overall effectiveness as a student. This correlation with school success was also more important than academic performance, class size, yearly expenditure per pupil, or level of teacher preparation. As self-esteem increases, so do academic achievement scores; as self-esteem decreases, so does achievement.

A recent Gallup Poll revealed that only 25% of all adults feel purposeful in their work, and even fewer feel an overall satisfaction with their life! Those who did express satisfaction said they were working toward two or more goals that were important to them. Likewise, children who feel purposeful are more outgoing and more assured. These children develop stronger, more mature friendships, and they are more likely to join peer groups who are worthy of their friendship. High self-esteem students are also more likely to develop good relationships with their teachers and to participate in extracurricular activities. These factors make the school experience more enjoyable and help students withstand the ups and downs involved with the challenge of learning.

Helping Students to Set and Achieve Worthwhile Goals

One way of helping students develop a sense of mission is to help them determine what *is* worthwhile, and then draw up a plan of action for accomplishing it. This means helping students to set and achieve goals. Children with goals are vibrant students *because* they have found something purposeful they want to do. They have a sense of where they are going.

Learning to achieve goals develops a beneficial behavior pattern.

A goal is like having a map. It helps you choose the direction you want to go, so you know where to focus your time and energy. When a student learns how to work toward an identified goal, he soon establishes a pattern to behave in a certain way. If a child rides a bike along a particular path to school often enough, it becomes a habit, and he follows it without even thinking, knowing it will lead to his destination. When students have *worthwhile* goals, they feel purposeful, and they are busy working toward something important.

Having goals ensures some success because the student is channeling his efforts in a single direction. Best of all, success in one area often leads to success in other areas. And that's the whole idea. Maybe you've heard a parent say, "My son is a poor student until football season, but his goal to be a part of the team motivates him during the football season into getting passing grades, because he has to maintain certain grades to stay eligible for the team. And when he applies himself, he does get good grades. Unfortunately, when the football season is over, he sets virtually no goals. He's back to being a reluctant student."

Having Goals Gives Children's Lives Meaning

Can your students set and achieve goals? During the workshops I conduct for youth around the country, I frequently ask young people what brings meaning and purpose to their lives. Young people often confuse *purpose* with practical realities such as where they're going to college, where they'll live, or what they're going to do for a job. While that's misguided, it's a good place to start. I usually proceed from that point to help them realize that purpose is the vision of what they see for themselves rather than the practical steps it will take to achieve their vision. A typical response is like the one from a young man in a recent workshop in Montana. I asked a class of seniors in Missoula, Montana High School, to identify what each saw as being the purpose of his life, and when he had first discovered that purpose. Kevin told me he wanted to be a veterinarian. Here's his story:

Young people often confuse purpose with practical realities.

Kevin's Story

"One day when I was in the eighth grade, my mother and I were on our way to my soccer practice. Sprawling on the grass near a stop sign was a white cat licking itself as though it was hurt. I begged my mother to let me go over to look at the cat. Well, the cat was hurt quite badly, and I persuaded my mom to take it to a local animal hospital. The vet cared for the cat, and my mother was left with the bill for an animal we didn't know who owned — we had never seen this cat before! My mother paid the bill anyway!

"We took the cat home and I put it in my room, and shut the door. I sat down and began to cry. Here I was sitting on my bed, stroking this strange cat, and crying. I felt silly crying, but mostly I couldn't understand my feelings. But then I thought that the tears were about what a good feeling it was to have helped this wounded and helpless animal. So, I got up and went down the street and put up a sign that said, 'If you lost your cat, call this number.'

"As I was walking home, I crossed over to the other side of the street and as I looked down at the sidewalk, saw there a tall mustard plant in full bloom. For some reason, it triggered something. The moment I gazed at the flower, I knew right then that I wanted to be a vet. It was this cat incident that made me realize I was most happy when I was with animals. I realized that I was drawn to other people's pets and was always rescuing dogs and cats and birds and bringing them home. I felt most honorable when I was in a care-taking role with animals. This whole incident just mirrored back, in a big way, what captured my attention most, and what made me feel the most satisfied. I can still see the crack in the sidewalk at the moment I decided that I was going to build a career out of helping animals. I saw myself first in a small practice, then a bigger one, and then in an animal hospital that I had built.

"Well, someone did come for the cat — a guy who lived not more than two blocks away — and I felt even better that I had helped out. But I still have a soft spot in my heart for that cat. And you know, the cat still comes around to visit now and then. I think he's grateful. He knows. I think animals know when we help them. I took a psychology course just to get some insight into my idea. I think being a vet will be a very important way to spend my life. I'm a senior now, and I still have my heart set on being a vet."

I asked Kevin if he had ever changed his mind about that goal. "Absolutely not. Never!" he replied instantly. "I've written many term papers about the subject, and I work part-time in a pet store, and I've taken the courses I'll need to get into college so I can do it. No, I'm very sure I'm going to be a vet."

I met Kevin's mother that evening in a program the school sponsored for parents. I was curious about her side of the story, and I wanted to see if Kevin had ever swayed from that goal. "Oh yes," she replied. "When he was a second-semester junior, he didn't know if he wanted to be a large animal vet, or a small animal vet! Other than that, I'd say no. But what I remember most from that incident is that it changed Kevin in many ways. Here was this child, an unmotivated learner who was sometimes reluctant to go to school. I had to rouse him several times in the morning to get him out of bed! Sometimes I had to get mean with him just to get him to do his homework. He didn't have many friends, and he wasn't all that excited about sports either. But, from that day on, he was *on fire*. He was so motivated. He studied, he got along well with his teachers, he was elected co-captain of the soccer team, he was more interesting to talk to and be with, and other kids began inviting him to their homes. It was just the most incredible thing. From that day on, Kevin had a reason for doing things and taking charge of his life. It was heartwarming. It was wonderful.

"My husband and I have three children and Kevin had been the difficult child. I'm embarrassed to say it, but there were so many times that I just didn't like my son all that much, and I felt awful that a mother could feel this way. When Kevin had a purpose, though, he had conviction. I respect and greatly admire my son. Kevin is a wonderful young man."

Help students examine what contributions they can make.

This story is not at all uncommon in terms of a major attitudinal shift that comes when a child's life takes on meaning. Although parents are the initial key, you are influential, too. You can help your students develop a sense of purpose by teaching them to think through the meaning they want to attach to life. Help students examine what contributions they'll make through their work. Do students know themselves? Ask students to pay attention to what captures their attention, and then to examine those interests. Help students learn to set meaningful goals so they can work toward them in a systematic way.

Whether you are teaching third grade or eleventh grade, you can help students learn the cycle of setting and achieving goals. Goals stem from dreams and desires, and that's where you need to start. To help your students set goals that are meaningful enough to get them to want to carry them out, here are some things you can do:

1. Inspire hope. I suggest you read one book every two or three months to your students. Read the biographies of exemplary people. Point out how these individuals were ordinary people who possessed the character, values, and dedication to achieve their goal, and that this, more than anything, was their real strength. Try to identify the particular turning point in these people's lives. For example, Janice was taken to the ballet by her parents when she was just a child, and said, "That's it, that's what I want to be." From the experience of seeing a wounded cat receive care, Kevin discovered he wanted to be a veterinarian.

2. Ask the student to observe what captures his attention. A key to helping students set goals is to center goals around what captures their attention. We all do better in those things that interest us. In Physical Education class, a student might be good at volleyball because he likes it. But how good is he at baseball or square dancing? Have you ever been involved in a project and suddenly several hours have passed and you didn't even realize it? Ask students to watch for those times when they are so absorbed or involved in a project that nothing else seems to matter. They concentrate on that one thing because it is of great interest. Here are other questions to ask: When they're looking for a book in the library, what do they pick up and read? What informational programs do they enjoy watching on television? What class do they really enjoy? What activities do they most enjoy doing? When they feel completely absorbed in something, what are they doing? Take class time where you examine the answers to these questions so students will have a better composite picture of their interests. Then talk with students about these areas of interest. Are they aware of them? How do these interests lend themselves for achieving purposeful goals?

3. Help students turn desires into goals. At first, students will have many different ideas about what they want, so you need to help them select two or three specific wants or desires. The next step is to turn a desire into a goal. The goal may be broad and general, such as "I want a new bike," "I want a car," "I want to get an A," or "I want to be a veterinarian." Help students examine their desires from every aspect to see which ones are really important. Say, "Yes, you want to be on the soccer team this year, but you don't sound very convincing. How much do you want to be a part of the team? Why is that important to you? What are you doing to make sure you get on the team?" Young people work harder and apply more enthusiasm toward goals that are important to them. If sports excite the student, have him read stories of athletes, or visit with professional athletes, or subscribe to magazines that highlight the challenges of the "thrill of victory and the agony of defeat." He'll discover that athletes practice two, three, or more hours a day, sometimes giving up other interests because being the best at their sport is usually their No. 1 goal. In other words, achieving a goal requires dedication and an intensity of purpose.

4. Help students find meaning. Help students puzzle over the *big* questions: "Who am I?" "What am I going to do with my life?" "What is happiness?" "Are my friendships forever?" "What's the purpose of life — is it more

> Teach your students to turn their desires into goals.

than to accrue financial success in the early years so you can retire and travel in the later years?" "Is life a journey or a destination?" These are thought-provoking questions. While answering these questions is a personal journey for each of us, helping youth ask and address them guides them in their search for answers.

Help your students address life's "big" questions.

5. Share your story. You can help students construct the framework for caring and meaning. How did *you* learn what the purpose was in your life? What is your story? What provided the initial framework for what you eventually defined as purposeful? Today, many children do not have the reference of two parents living and working together. There are many single parents trying to do it all alone, and many parents who had a less than idyllic background, who themselves came from a family torn by pain. Family life does not have to be perfect for us to draw strength from it. Talk about this with your students. Tell them how you overcame the obstacles to develop your own personality, character, and morality. Were you an A-student in high school? Did you put yourself through college? Did you struggle in your first few years on the job? What did you overcome? Did you develop into a person of character and conviction? Tell them how you managed to do this. I work with so many youth and families where children have little if any sense of purpose for their lives. In this time of family chaos and impermanence, it's important to talk with our students about what brings meaning to life and help them make sense of it all.

I find that in this time of rapid social change there are many families where lives are torn apart by family hurts and pain, separation and divorce. I see many adults busy defining their lives by material success and rewards, or working hours that are not conducive to building the lives of their children. The result is that many children are physically homeless and emotionally bankrupt. And if they aren't, they know of other children who are. Unfortunately, it seems to happen to more and more of our students.

One of the greatest gifts you will ever give your students is the spirit and willingness to go forward in a positive, purposeful, and loving way. Adults help youth define purpose.

Nine Key Areas for Goal Setting

There are nine key areas that help give meaning to our lives. Talk with students about their goals in each of these areas, why they are important, and what their plans are for bringing these goals about.

- **Goals for peace of mind**: The search for meaning and spiritual fulfillment.
- **Personal Relationships:** Goals to improve relationships with parents, friends, teachers, and others.
- **Learning and Education:** What would you like to know more about?
- **Status and Respect:** To which groups do you want to belong? From whom do you want respect?

- **Leisure Time:** What activities, hobbies, sports, or travel opportunities would you like to learn more about? To do more?

- **Fitness:** Goals for physical fitness and overall health.

- **Money Needs:** Goals for having enough money to do the things you want to do.

- **Work Goals:** What kind of job path will you choose? What are your goals for productive work and career success?

- **Others:** Goals that may not fit into the previous categories.

How to Help Students Accomplish Goals

Six Questions to Direct Goal Setting

It's unlikely that all students will set goals and work toward accomplishing them just because you suggest it. The following questions can help you effectively guide students toward goal achievement.

1. Has the student made the goal his own? If a student doesn't really want something, it's unlikely he'll make the commitment needed to accomplish it! He'll give up when faced with hard work. He needs to *own* the goal. If you try to convince him to set a goal you would like to see attained (for example, you want him to do better work in your classroom), you have to help him see it as his own goal, otherwise he won't be motivated to achieve it. If you want him to be a good student, that's one thing. But if *he* wants to be a good student, that's another. He's likely to be a good student because that is *his* goal, too. He has to have an inner fire, a drive that says, "It's important to *me*."

Students must want to achieve the goal for themselves.

2. Is the goal attainable? Does the student believe he can meet his goal? Is it achievable? That doesn't mean that it has to be easy, but there has to be a better than 50-50 chance he can meet the goal. You don't want a goal that is self-defeating, one so difficult he almost certainly will not achieve it. The goal must be one he personally believes he can achieve. Moreover, the goal has to be a challenge. There's a saying that goes, "Most people don't aim too high and miss, they aim too low and hit!" The same is true for students if they set goals that are yours and not theirs, or if the goal is too easy. If a student sets a goal to get at least a "C" on her paper and she knows she can do better, what's the challenge? If her goal is to do at least 20 sit-ups and she can already do 19 with no problem, what's the challenge?

3. What makes the goal worth achieving? What are the benefits? Is it worth the time and effort? When you are lecturing, and you say, "Now, this next material will not be on the test, but you should know it anyway," what do your students do? Do they pay as much attention as they normally would, or do they exchange a grin with friends, sit back, and relax? They probably just kick back and take it easy. They don't take the material seriously, because they know they won't be tested on it. They assume there's little benefit to taking notes and paying attention.

4. Has he put his goal in writing? When the student writes his goal down, it makes it clear in his mind, and helps him get organized. It makes for a plan of attack. And, the student sees his progress when he can cross off a written goal. The student internalizes his goal and buys into *his* commitment when he puts pencil to paper. If the goal is just in his head, he can easily forget about it. We have thousands of thoughts daily and most are forgotten in moments. But those we take the time and effort to focus on matter more.

Goals are a blueprint for achieving success.

Suppose you hire an architect to build your house. He meets with you and says, "I have a lot of great ideas. I'll put the master bedroom with high ceilings here, I'll put the jacuzzi here, I'll put the living room here . . ." You listen a while, then say, "I'm having trouble remembering and visualizing all this. May I see your blueprints please?" The architect smiles at you and says, "Blueprints? I never write anything down. I keep it all in my head!" Would you let this person build your house? Probably not. Even if the architect is a genius, no one can work without a blueprint. The same is true for goals. Writing them down provides a blueprint for your efforts. Ask the child to post the goal where he can see it. Otherwise, *his* shortsightedness may cause him to forget. I talk with many students who set goals, but by the end of the week, they've lost sight of them! Have the student make several copies and post them where he can see them on his mirror, on his notebook, and on the inside of his locker.

5. Are the deadlines realistic? Teach students how to break long-term goals into short-term goals. For example, if getting into college is the long-term goal, in order to reach it, the student will need to break it down into a series of short-term goals, ranging from doing well in each of her classes to getting the money together for tuition. Goals and deadlines are easier to reach when they are broken down into manageable tasks. Help your students set dates for each goal, major and minor. Some dates are predetermined. If a student is going to take the SAT college admission exam, for example, he has to adjust to the test schedule. But he can still set intermediate deadlines, such as the goal to have the vocabulary learned by this date, the math by that date, and so on. Having a written deadline motivates the student and helps him manage the task. It also helps him prioritize where and how he will allocate his time. Then, when he sees he's nearing a deadline, he can push himself just a little harder, or know when to plan downtime and play-time. When the student accomplishes his goal within the deadline, he feels successful.

Make sure a student doesn't set overly ambitious deadlines. You want the student to experience success, not failure. Don't let a child put down that she's going to make 10 new friends this month if she's a very shy person who has trouble making two friends a year. Don't encourage an "A" as her goal in math, if she's not even getting "C's" now.

6. When the goal is achieved what is the reward? Let's say a student has set a goal and accomplished it. He did something he set his mind to do, and now he deserves to be proud of himself. He can take the time to feel the satisfaction of having accomplished something purposeful. Teach him to do something nice for himself as a reward. Ask him, "What one nice thing will you do for yourself, because you have been diligent and hard at work on your goal?" Maybe it's a few days of downtime, or a new item of clothing, or tickets to a special concert. Rewards are a form of praise. The specific reward should be generated by your student for his own accomplishments.

Turning Obstacles into Opportunities

Perhaps some students seem to have no striking motivation, no drive, or any desire to set goals. A student may say he just doesn't know what he wants, or what he's good at. We all know students sometimes give excuses for why they can't do something. Whether it's "Goals aren't important," or "I don't know how," or "Someone might make fun of me," or "I might fail," your students have a number of reasons for their reluctance to set goals. Teach them to view obstacles as opportunities.

A friend of mine illustrates this concept by telling the story of a farmer who grew bored with farming and decided to seek his fortune in a gold mine. After selling his farm, he went to Alaska and searched for gold. He was gone many years and had all sorts of adventures. But he never found gold, and he spent most of his life being poor. Finally, exhausted and out of hope, he traveled back to see his former farm. To his amazement, he found a mansion where the farmhouse had been. The former farmland had been beautifully groomed and landscaped.

He knocked on the door. The new owner answered. "What on earth happened here?" asked the bewildered former farmer. "You barely had enough money to buy the farm from me, as I remember. How did you get so rich?"

The new owner just smiled. "Actually, it was all due to you. There were diamonds on this property, acres and acres of diamonds!"

The old farmer scoffed. "Diamonds! I knew every inch of this land, and there were no diamonds here."

The new owner nodded, and pulled from his pocket a lump of what looked like coal. "I carry around this small one as a good-luck charm. Here is one of the diamonds from this property."

The farmer was amazed. "That's a diamond? I remember seeing a lot of those all over this land. I used to swear at them and kick them because they got in the way when I was plowing. I thought they were lumps of coal! That doesn't look anything like a diamond to me!"

You see, the farmer didn't recognize the diamonds when he saw them. Not

Goals and deadlines need to be broken down into manageable tasks.

Not all opportunities look like diamonds.

all opportunities look like diamonds. In their unpolished form, diamonds look like lumps of coal. Help students recognize the diamonds in their lives, those they may not recognize right now.

Goal-setting leads to achievement and a sense of purpose and fulfillment, and it contributes to a high level of self-esteem. Students with high self-esteem seek the stimulation of demanding goals. Moreover, reaching demanding goals nurtures good self-esteem. Students with low self-esteem seek the safety of the familiar and undemanding. Being confined to the familiar and undemanding further weakens self-esteem. It's our responsibility to teach goal-setting. As students see goals met, they build confidence and demand more of themselves.

Discussion

1. Why is a sense of mission or purpose important to students of all ages? How does purpose affect self-esteem?

2. How can teachers help their students to identify what is important to them and set realistic goals?

3. How can educators aid their students in achieving those goals? How should we deal with a frustrated student who seems to be making no progress?

Chapter 14

BECOMING AN EFFECTIVE EDUCATOR:
Developing Your Educational Philosophy

*Children spend a significant amount of time, as well as their
most formative years, in the school environment.*

By understanding the importance of self-esteem and knowing what it entails, educators can be a significant link in helping students develop high self-esteem. Most importantly, by creating an environment that supports, reinforces, and strengthens self-esteem, we can help students develop habits that lead to having healthy and functional lives as adults.

There's a difference between getting a high school diploma and attaining a meaningful education. In our world of increasing choices and options, our children face, in every direction, frontiers of limitless possibilities. They need to exercise independent judgment, and take responsibility for the choices, values, and actions that shape their lives.

We can no longer afford to rearrange the chairs on the Titanic. We must examine our values, evaluate our goals, and find ways to bring about our highest visions for students. The question is *What do we really want?* As a parent, and a consultant to American schools, I continue to hear what I call a "new educational consciousness." I couldn't be more optimistic about this.

Our workplaces need individuals who have a healthy sense of self-esteem.

What parents everywhere are beginning to express, is that in addition to acquiring the skills of reading, writing, and learning, they want their children to gain *self-knowledge.* We want our children to know themselves so well that they're able to turn their joys into their jobs and their toys into their tools. We want them to experience productive and meaningful work based on their inner desires and talents. We want them to be in mutually satisfying and loving relationships, those in which they will not be hurt emotionally or physically. Nor do we want them to hurt the people whom they love. We want them to be in good health and be fit. We want them to discover the connection between self-responsibility and happiness, and to care about their own emotional well-being. We want them to be compassionate people who are able to nurture and sustain friendships. We want them to set and achieve *worthwhile* goals. Above all, we want them to live a life characterized by meaning. For the educator, it's a matter of doing the right things, or doing things right.

Are You an Effective Educator?

It's a matter of doing the right things and doing things right.

Think about the teachers you had in school, the ones you liked and those you didn't, and ask yourself these questions.

- Did some manage to involve you in the subject they were teaching and make you *want* to learn?

- Did some exude warmth and compassion?

- Did some exude vitality and excellence?

- Did certain teachers make you feel you could ask them anything you wanted about their subject?

- Did the best teachers make you think and participate in class rather than allow you to hide behind the boy sitting in front of you and sneak peeks at the wall clock to see how much time was left?

- Were some teachers so exciting that you looked forward to their classes?

- Did a few of your teachers talk *with* students rather than lecture *at* them day after day?

- Did you notice that in some classes time flew by because you were busy every minute rather than playing with your pencil and daydreaming while waiting for the class to start or for the teacher to hand out and collect homework?

- Did the best teachers treat all students as part of the class rather than ignore the slow students because they were going to do poorly or ignore the smart ones because they could take care of themselves?

If you can answer yes to many of these questions, then you are remembering effective educators — those who helped you become a "real person," and to learn the "real stuff." Effective educators come in a variety of sizes and shapes, and they possess different personalities and teaching methods and styles, but they share certain characteristics. Among them:

■ **Effective educators don't write off any student.** Good teachers don't have one set of standards for good students and lower standards for others. They know that students learn at different rates. Some students are quicker than others, and some need more help in understanding the lesson. Good teachers are convinced that all students can learn. These educators believe there's more to their job than to see that all students achieve the course proficiency requirements. Effective educators have high expectations for all their students and strive to help them fulfill their potential. They know that students who are expected to do well in school usually succeed, while those who are expected to fail usually do so.

■ **Effective educators know the importance of praise as a motivator.** Good teachers don't take for granted good behavior or success, nor do they comment only on misbehavior or failure. Successful teachers continually encourage their students, and provide experiences where each student achieves a measure of success.

■ **Effective educators create an atmosphere conducive to living and learning.** A classroom needn't be absent of conflict to be dysfunctional. Warmth and enthusiasm for the subjects taught often go together. Good educators make subjects come alive, and simultaneously make all students feel appreciated.

■ **Effective educators use class time well.** Good teachers have a commitment to learning, not just teaching. They develop creative and stimulating lesson plans, and through a series of teaching methodologies test for student learning. They know that if students are not learning, they need to find alternative ways in which students *do* succeed in learning.

■ **Effective educators establish clear boundaries for students.** Good teachers delineate only those rules and procedures that are conducive to keeping students physically and emotionally safe, and are consistent and fair when reinforcing them.

■ **Effective educators seize learning opportunities.** Good teachers encourage all their students to contribute. They are willing to move the class in a new direction if it seems to be more understandable and interesting to their students.

■ **Effective educators have a clearly defined philosophy.** Good teachers know that in order to focus on those things that are the most valuable, they need to have a philosophy to guide their actions.

Good teachers have a commitment to learning, not just teaching.

Of course, you could add many other characteristics to this list, and you should. But let's zero in on the last point, the importance of clarifying our beliefs about the purpose and goals of educating children — a *philosophy*. This philosophy is one that exists outside of the school district's mission statements, and apart from the individual school's goals and objectives for the year.

The Role of Philosophy in Your Teaching Life

At the heart of purposeful activity in teaching is an educational philosophy that helps educators address value-laden questions and make decisions. An educational philosophy suggests purpose in education, clarifies objectives and activities, suggests learning theories, defines the curriculum, and guides the selection of strategies for teaching. Your philosophy articulates what *you* want from your teaching, and specifies the activities needed for working with youth. It defines and clarifies your role and guides your strategies. There are many ways to teach. Curriculum decisions ultimately reflect differing beliefs and values about what we see as important values to pass on to our students.

What are your beliefs about education? Have you solidified your values so that you can make decisions for your students and for their learning?

The Benefits of an Educational Philosophy

Here are some of the benefits you can achieve by consciously choosing an educational philosophy. The following list is just a beginning. You can add your own thoughts. The idea is that you see the value of carefully thinking through and evaluating a philosophy that will guide your actions and enable you to be more effective and satisfied in your role as an educator.

Your philosophy articulates what you want from your teaching.

- With a philosophy, I can look at ideas about teaching that are reactive and determine those values that I really want to impart and the ones I want to change.

- I force myself to think about what is important to teach and this guides my actions.

- I become more aware of my strengths — how much I have to offer students and how much I can share. This gives me courage and confidence to pull through the tough and challenging times.

- I set goals for myself as an educator and have concrete objectives. This helps me change what I don't like about my teaching and set new standards.

- I become more clear about what I really want for my students and what I actually give each one.

- I become more aware of my own repressed but natural resentments about teaching, such as the lack of freedom and the sacrifices that must be made. I am able to acknowledge these resentments in a healthy manner.

The Search for a Philosophical Attitude

Schooling is a moral venture, one that necessitates choosing specific values from among innumerable possibilities. Each educator must address some difficult questions about the purpose of schooling, and his or her role in working with students. These questions include asking:

- What is education for?

- What should the school accept responsibility for?

- What kind of citizens and what kind of society do we want?

- What methods of instruction or classroom organization must we provide to produce these desired ends?

- Is the purpose of school to change, adapt to, or accept the social order?

- What objectives should be common to all students?

- Should objectives deal with controversial issues, or only those things for which there is established knowledge?

- Should objectives be based on the needs of society in general, or the expressed needs of students?

The Five Educational Philosophies and What They Mean

There are five distinct educational philosophies: perennialism, idealism, realism, experimentalism, and existentialism. Collectively, these philosophies represent a broad spectrum of thought about what schools should be and what they should do. As the following definitions illustrate, educators holding differing philosophies each would create very different schools, each with a distinct atmosphere.

1. Perennialism. The most conservative, traditional, or inflexible of the five philosophies is perennialism. Perennialists believe that education should focus on developing rationality. Students should be taught through structured study. Perennialists favor a curriculum of subjects, taught through highly disciplined drills and behavior-control. The teacher interprets and tells. The student is a passive recipient.

2. Idealism. This philosophy espouses that reality is a world within a person's mind. Teachers are models of ideal behavior. The function of schools is to sharpen intellectual processes. Students in such schools have a somewhat passive role, receiving and memorizing the reporting of the teacher. Change in the school program is generally considered an intrusion on the orderly process of things.

3. Realism. For the realist, the job of schools is to teach students about the world. The realist favors a school dominated by subjects of the here-and-now world, such as math and science. Students are taught factual information for mastery. The teacher imparts knowledge to students. Classrooms are highly ordered and disciplined, students are possible participants in the study of things.

4. Experimentalism. The experimentalist openly accepts change, for the world is an ever-changing place. The experimentalist favors a school with heavy emphasis on social subjects and experiences. Learning occurs through a problem-solving or inquiry format. Teachers aid or consult with learners who are actively involved in discovering and experiencing the world.

5. Existentialism. The existentialist believes that change is natural and necessary. Schools are to assist students in understanding themselves and learning about their place in society. If subject matter exists, it is a matter of interpretation, such as the arts, ethics, or philosophy. Teacher-student interaction centers around assisting students in their personal learning quests.

The following self-scoring test will enable you to assess your preferred educational philosophy.

These five philosophies represent a broad spectrum of thought about what schools should do.

Philosophy Preference Assessment

© Jon Wiles, Joseph C. Bondi, 1984. Reprinted with permission.

Directions: For each item below, respond according to the strength of your belief, scoring the item on a scale of 1-5. A one (1) indicates strong disagreement, a five (5) indicates strong agreement.

1 2 3 4 5   **(1)** Ideal teachers are constant questioners.

1 2 3 4 5   **(2)** Schools exist for societal improvement.

1 2 3 4 5   **(3)** Teaching should center around the inquiry technique.

1 2 3 4 5   **(4)** Demonstration and recitation are essential components of learning.

1 2 3 4 5   **(5)** Students should always be permitted to determine their own rules in the educational process.

1 2 3 4 5   **(6)** Reality is spiritual and rational.

1 2 3 4 5   **(7)** Curriculum should be based on the laws of natural science.

1 2 3 4 5   **(8)** The teacher should be a strong authority figure in the classroom.

1 2 3 4 5   **(9)** The student is a receiver of knowledge.

1 2 3 4 5   **(10)** Ideal teachers interpret knowledge.

1 2 3 4 5   **(11)** Lecture-discussion is the most effective teaching technique.

1 2 3 4 5   **(12)** Institutions should seek avenues toward self-improvement through an orderly process.

1 2 3 4 5   **(13)** Schools are obligated to teach moral truths.

1 2 3 4 5   **(14)** School programs should focus on social problems and issues.

1 2 3 4 5   **(15)** Institutions exist to preserve and strengthen spiritual and social values.

1 2 3 4 5   **(16)** Subjective opinion reveals truth.

1 2 3 4 5   **(17)** Teachers are seen as facilitators of learning.

1 2 3 4 5   **(18)** Schools should be educational "smorgasbords."

1 2 3 4 5   **(19)** Memorization is the key to process skills.

1 2 3 4 5   **(20)** Reality consists of objects.

1 2 3 4 5   **(21)** Schools exist to foster the intellectual process.

1 2 3 4 5   **(22)** Schools foster an orderly means for change.

1 2 3 4 5   **(23)** There are essential skills everyone must learn.

1 2 3 4 5   **(24)** Teaching by subject area is the most effective approach.

1 2 3 4 5   **(25)** Students should play an active part in program design and evaluation.

1 2 3 4 5   **(26)** A functioning member of society follows rules of conduct.

1 2 3 4 5   **(27)** Reality is rational.

1 2 3 4 5   **(28)** Schools should reflect the society they serve.

1 2 3 4 5   **(29)** The teacher should set an example for the students.

1 2 3 4 5 **(30)** The most effective learning does not take place in a highly structured, strictly disciplined environment.

1 2 3 4 5 **(31)** The curriculum should be based on unchanging spiritual truths.

1 2 3 4 5 **(32)** The most effective learning is nonstructured.

1 2 3 4 5 **(33)** Truth is a constant expressed through ideas.

1 2 3 4 5 **(34)** Drill and factual knowledge are important components of any learning environment.

1 2 3 4 5 **(35)** Societal consensus determines morality.

1 2 3 4 5 **(36)** Knowledge is gained primarily through the senses.

1 2 3 4 5 **(37)** There are essential pieces of knowledge that everyone should know.

1 2 3 4 5 **(38)** The school exists to facilitate self-awareness.

1 2 3 4 5 **(39)** Change is an ever-present process.

1 2 3 4 5 **(40)** Truths are best taught through the inquiry process.

Philosophy Assessment Scoring

The following sets of questions relate to the five philosophies of education:

Perennialist — 6, 8, 10, 13, 15, 31, 34, 37

Idealist — 9, 11, 19, 21, 24, 27, 29, 33

Realist — 4, 7, 12, 20, 22, 23, 26, 28

Experimentalist — 2, 3, 14, 17, 25, 35, 39, 40

Existentialist — 1, 5, 16, 18, 30, 32, 36, 38

Scoring Steps

1. Taking these questions by set (e.g., the eight perennialist questions), record the value of the answer given (i.e., Strongly disagree =1). Total the numerical value of each set. In a single set of numbers, the total should fall between 8 (all 1's) and 40 (all 5's).

2. Divide the total score fore each set by five (Example 40/5 = 8).

3. Plot the scores.

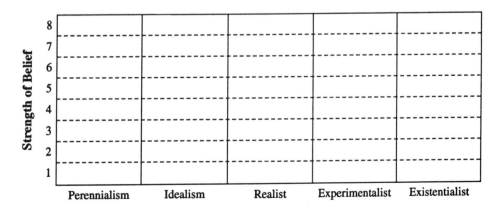

Interpretation

Having plotted your responses on the grid, you now have a profile which gives you an idea of your beliefs about schools. Some patterns are common and therefore subject to interpretation.

Pattern 1. If your profile on the response grid is basically flat, reflecting approximately the same score for each set of questions, it indicates an inability to discriminate in terms of preference.

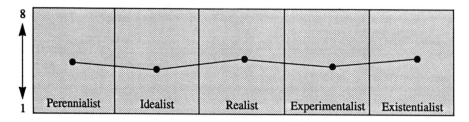

Pattern 2. If your pattern is generally a slanting line across the grid, then you show a strong structured or nonstructured orientation in your reported beliefs.

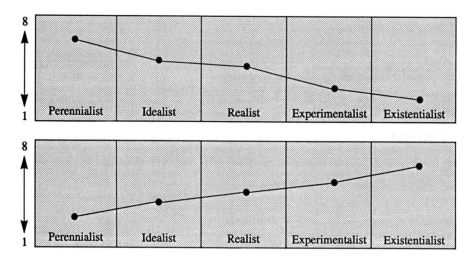

Pattern 3. If your pattern appears as a bimodal or trimodal distribution (two or three peaks), it indicates indecisiveness on crucial issues and suggests the need for further clarification. The closer the peaks (adjacent sets), the less contradiction in the responses.

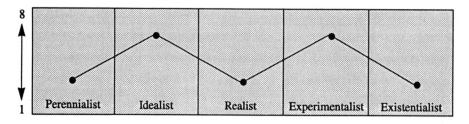

Pattern 4. If the pattern appears U-shaped, a significant amount of value inconsistency is indicated. Such a response would suggest strong beliefs in very different and divergent systems.

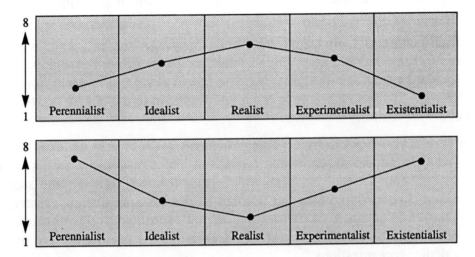

Pattern 5. A pattern which is simply a flowing curve without sharp peaks and valleys may suggest either an eclectic philosophy, or a person only beginning to study his or her own philosophy.

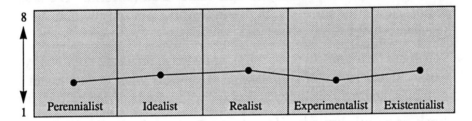

Your Philosophy Is Showing!

Classroom space, organization and dissemination of knowledge, uses of learning materials, instructional styles, teaching strategies, organization of students, discipline, and student roles are all indicators of your educational philosophy.

Classroom organization. Traditionally, the room is arranged in such a way that all attention is on the teacher. With this arrangement, there is little opportunity for lateral communication. Activity is "fixed" by the arrangement of furniture. The conditions are perfect for teacher lecture but little else. Another possibility is to create multi-purpose spaces with the focus of attention generally in the center of the classroom. This style simultaneously permits increased student involvement, mobility, and varied learning activities. It does not focus attention solely on the teacher.

Student mobility. The movement of students is another subtle indicator of your philosophy. Movement in some classrooms is totally dependent upon the teacher. Students in such a classroom must request permission to talk, go to the restroom, or approach the teacher. In a less stationary classroom, limited movement is possible. Students may be able to sharpen pencils or get supplies without prior teacher approval.

Most programs employ one of three standard curriculum designs.

Organization of knowledge. Your philosophy also determines the way you organize and disseminate knowledge. Most programs of study employ one of three standard curriculum designs: *building-blocks design, branching design,* or *spiral design.* It is also possible to order knowledge in terms of *task accomplishment* or *simple learning processes.*

- **Building-blocks design:** This structure takes a clearly defined body of knowledge and orders it into a pyramid-like arrangement. Students are taught foundational material, which leads to more complex and specialized knowledge. The end product of the learning design, mastery, is known in advance. Activities that do not contribute to this directed path are not allowed. Building-blocks designs are the most structured of curriculum organizations.

- **Branching pattern:** This variation incorporates limited choice in learning. Branching prescribes the eventual outcomes of the learning program, although the prescription is multiple rather than uniform. The branching design allows for some variability in learning but only within tightly defined boundaries.

- **Spiral curriculum:** In this design, knowledge areas are continually revisited at higher levels of complexity. It controls what is taught and predetermines the time the students are exposed to the knowledge to be learned.

- **Task accomplishment:** Here the purpose of the learning experience is predetermined, but student interaction is flexible. Competency-based skill continuums are an example of this design.

- **Teaching processes:** Here knowledge is simply a medium for teaching processes. Thus, reading could be taught regardless of the particular material used by the student.

Instructional Orientation. Your educational philosophy also influences your instructional style. In some classrooms, learning is completely structured. The teacher controls the flow of data, communication, and assessment. Slightly more flexible is a pattern of didactic teaching whereby the teacher delivers information, controls the exchange of ideas, and enforces the correct conclusions through a question-and-answer session. Or the teacher can allow the free exchange of ideas in the classroom but enforce a standardized summation of the process. Still more flexible is a pattern where students are allowed to experience a learning process and then draw their own conclusions about meaning.

Teaching Strategies. The teaching strategies found in classrooms often provide clues about the teacher's educational philosophy. Two behaviors that speak louder than words about the learning strategy employed in the classroom are the *motivational techniques* being used, and the *interactive distances* between the teacher and student.

Motivational techniques. Teachers can use a range of motivational techniques.

- **Threats.** Teachers who use threats or fear as a motivator generally seek maximum structure in the classroom.

- **Coercion.** As a rule, coercion arrests behavior and encourages conformity to previous patterns of behavior.

- **Extrinsic rewards.** Whether immediate or deferred, extrinsic rewards also encourage structure by linking the desired behavior with reward.

- **Intrinsic rewards.** Whether immediate or deferred, intrinsic rewards have the opposite effect. Intrinsic rewards encourage student participation in the reward system and thereby result in a wider range of acceptable behaviors.

Intrinsic rewards encourage student participation in the reward system.

Interactive distance. Another dimension of the learning strategy in a classroom setting is the interactive distance between the teacher and students.

Organization of students. Your educational philosophy also determines the way you organize your students. You can group students according to their age, or by a more flexible criterion, such as subject area. Another choice that offers still greater flexibility groups students within grades and subjects according to capacity. Even greater organizational flexibility is found in schools that group students by needs and student interests.

Disciplinary measures. Discipline techniques used to influence student behavior are determined by our educational philosophy. For some teachers, all infractions are given the same treatment regardless of severity. For those teachers, there is a hierarchy of discipline measures to deal with different discipline problems. Sometimes severe or recurrent discipline problems are the only ones that receive attention. Where great flexibility is found, the pattern for discipline is sometimes unclear because discipline measures are unevenly applied. Some teachers practice no observable discipline measures!

Student roles. Like teachers, students hold a role-perception of who they are and what they can do in a classroom setting. A question that usually receives a telling response for an observer in a classroom is, "How do students learn in this classroom?" The following suggests the potential range of responses to such a question:

- They recite and copy from board.
- They listen, take notes, take tests.
- They listen, read, question, take tests.
- They work on things, read.
- They do things that interest them.

Discussion

1. What were your original reasons for becoming a teacher? How have these changed over the years?

2. Can you change your educational philosophy? How?

3. What philosophy is needed to provide youth with the very best education — one that will sustain them throughout their lives?

Chapter 15

TAKING ON THE CHALLENGE:
Putting Self-Esteem on Your Agenda

Education is the most important profession, because
through the hands of educators pass all professions.

Children Learn What They Live

Teaching has never been more challenging — or more rewarding — than it is today. Our changing social climate demands that students leave school equipped with knowledge and the ability to apply that knowledge in their work and personal lives. The realities of teaching include tight budgets, full classrooms, complex materials, and the need for teachers to connect, one-on-one, with their students, in spite of the challenges. Like you, sometimes it seems to me that we cannot do enough. Certainly, teachers must cope with many demands — demands on their skills, compassion, time, and effort. Some may think it's too much to ask teachers to focus on developing their students' self-esteem. Yet, teachers must take on the challenge.

As we have seen, a high self-esteem results in improved student performance and achievement. High self-esteem students pose fewer discipline problems, which frees the teacher to spend more time teaching and less time maintaining order. This, then, is the first benefit that teachers receive from helping their students improve their self-esteem. After all, one of the great rewards of teaching is seeing your students learn! There are many others.

By thinking about what we want for our students, we can help them develop a set of inner beliefs and outward skills that will serve them all their lives. In doing so, we discover just how much we learn about ourselves along the way. While we coach our students to discover their potential, we discover new strengths within ourselves. I know this has been true for me.

Although I am no longer in the public classroom, I taught for 11 years. I'm still a teacher at heart. I've held a university faculty post for six years and have served as director of an educational foundation. Now, as I lecture, sharing my time with people across the nation — parents, educators, and other professionals who work with youth — I am still teaching. Teaching has been the theme that has dominated my work, and I have found it enormously rewarding. In applying similar techniques that I have outlined in this book, I have learned much about myself and others. If what I have learned could be broken down into "lessons," the lessons would be as follows.

The 12 Lessons I Have Learned

1. Satisfaction. As a result of my efforts, I have seen young people prosper as they grow into intelligent, enlightened, and compassionate persons.

2. Empathy. In seeking to understand my students, I have had to put myself in their place, which means I have experienced the same excitement and frustrations of learning as my students.

3. Patience. I have come to understand that each student learns differently, in her own time, at her own pace. Learning is the key. Realizing that my teaching was only as good as the students' learning, I changed my emphasis from teaching to learning.

4. Endurance. I discovered an unknown reserve of strength within myself. I learned that I could juggle 33 students with 33 sets of needs as long as the classroom was a Cooperative Learning environment. I began to see teaching as exciting, challenging, and stimulating, but I also realized that to take on this job, I needed to be healthy and fit. Consequently, I began a rigorous weekly workout routine that has improved both my professional stamina and personal wellness.

5. Listening. I learned not only to listen to the voices of my students, but also to their feelings and the subtle clues buried in their behavior. I learned to hear what they were really saying, rather than what I would prefer to hear — and many times I was amazed how different the reality was from my expectations!

6. Responsibility. My goal is to make sure my students know they can count on me. I have learned to accept the duties and obligations of being an educator, *and* caretaker of an instrument as precious as a mind. I learned that I can be depended upon to fulfill my role as a teacher. Accepting the responsibility for my role has forced me to clarify my own values and has challenged me to uphold them.

7. Assertiveness. I learned the necessity of clear communications, which means providing sufficient detail and straightforward explanations. When you're a leader, it is essential to be assertive and consistent.

8. The needs of my students. By listening and observing, I can determine what my students need from me. I strive to have the wisdom to accept that their needs may be different than what I expected.

9. The nature of adults. Teaching youth has taught me much about the nature of adults. When you associate with children, you learn that children and adults often adopt similar roles to cope with stress. I have seen all types among my students — the clown, the show-off, the prima donna, the child who puts other kids down to build himself up. In watching children play out these roles, I realized that they shared one thing in common — they were all just a little bit scared of something. The same is true for adults who act out the roles of the clown, the bully, or the show-off. Knowing this has helped make it easier for me to understand adults.

10. Self-control and discipline. Teaching has taught me that I can take charge of my own life. When you're in charge, you learn quickly from your mistakes, you experience the pride that comes from accomplishing things, and you gain a deep sense of satisfaction. Teaching has taught me to exercise self-discipline in setting objectives and meeting goals and deadlines. I learned that I could help others acquire new responses to inappropriate behavior. Most of all, I learned to heed my own advice.

11. The value of self-esteem. From working with others, seven hours a day, I learned the value of self-esteem and its effect on daily performance, and its influence on the outcome of a student's life. I learned that when students don't feel worthy, they don't act as though they are worthy. When students don't care about themselves, they can't take on personal responsibilities that show they care for others. In my classrooms, I learned that self-esteem was the most important item on my agenda.

12. I learned to be a better person. My years of teaching have made me a better person. Children need us to model effective behavior — what we do is always more important than what we say we should do. By striving to be the loving, caring, enthusiastic person I want my students to become, I have learned to better accept myself as I am and not penalize myself for not being someone I am not.

You Are Important in Your Students' Lives

In both teaching and in day-to-day life, you can function at the survival level — just doing what it takes to get through another day — or you can create a creative, joyful, and positive experience. The choice is yours. Roadblocks and challenges will always crop up, but the choice of attitude is yours alone. Choosing the positive and joyful makes the journey a rewarding one for you *and* for the students who pass through your life. Many years ago, when I became a new parent, a friend gave me a framed version of this beautiful message. Although written for parents, it offers a time-honored application for all of us who work with formative minds. I urge you to keep these words in mind when you find yourself doubting that you are important to your students. You are important, because through you, your students can learn a better way to live.

Children Learn What They Live

If a child lives with criticism, he learns to condemn.

If a child lives with hostility, he learns to fight.

If a child lives with ridicule, he learns to be shy.

If a child lives with shame, he learns to feel guilty.

If a child lives with tolerance, he learns to be patient.

If a child lives with encouragement, he learns confidence.

If a child lives with praise, he learns to appreciate.

If a child lives with fairness, he learns justice.

If a child lives with security, he learns to have faith.

If a child lives with approval, he learns to like himself.

If a child lives with acceptance and friendship,

   he learns to find love in the world.

                                        Dorothy Law Nolte

I wish you joy and rewards in your lifework.

Bettie B. Youngs

Resources and Suggested Readings

Ackoff, R. *The Art of Problem Solving*. New York: John Wiley and Sons, 1978.

Anderson, E., G. Tedman, and C. Rogers. *Self-Esteem for Tots to Teens*. New York: Meadowbrook/Simon and Schuster, 1984.

Anglund, J. W. *A Friend Is Someone Who Likes You*. New York: Hartcourt and Brace, 1985.

Axline, V. M. *Dibs: In Search of Self*. New York: Ballantine Books, 1967.

Barksdale, L. S. *Essays on Self-Esteem*. Idyllwild, CA: The Barksdale Foundation, 1977.

Baron, J. B. and R. J. Sternberg, Robert J., Ed. *Teaching Thinking Skills: Theory and Practice*. New York: W. H. Freeman and Co. 1987.

Baron, J. D. *Kids and Drugs*. New York: Putnam, 1983.

Beane, J., and R. Lipka. *Self-Concept, Self-Esteem and the Curriculum*. New York: Teachers College Press, 1984.

Bedley, G. *The ABCD's of Discipline*. Irvine, CA: People-Wise Publications, 1979.

Bennett, W. *Schools Without Drugs*. U.S. Department of Education: White House, Washington, DC., 1989.

Bergstrom, C. *Losing Your Best Friend: Losing Friendship*. New York: Human Science Press, 1984.

Berne, E. *What Do You Say After You Say Hello?* New York: Grove Press, 1971.

Berne, P., and L. Savary. *Building Self-Esteem in Children*. New York: Continuum, 1989.

Bessell, H., and T. Kelly, Jr. *The Parent Book*. Rolling Hills Estates, CA: Jalmar Press, 1977.

Betancourt, J. *Am I Normal?* New York: Avon, 1983.

Bingham, E. E., and S. J. Stryker. *CHOICES: A Teen Woman's Journal for Self-Awareness and Personal Planning*. El Toro, CA: Mission Publications, 1985.

Bingham, E. E., and S. J. Stryker. *CHOICES: A Teen Man's Journal for Self-Awareness and Personal Planning*. El Toro, CA: Mission Publications, 1985.

Bloom, Benjamin S. "Affective Outcomes of School Learning." *Phi Delta Kappan* 1977: pp. 193-199.

Blume, J. *Are You There, God? It's Me, Margaret*. New York: Dell, 1970.

Blume, J. *Then Again, Maybe I Won't*. New York: Dell, 1971.

Booraem, C., J. Flowers, and B. Schwartz. *Help Your Children Be Self-Confident*. Englewood Cliffs, NJ: Prentice-Hall, Inc., 1978.

Bonny, H., and L. Savary. *Music and Your Mind*. New York: Harper & Row, 1973.

Borba, M. *Esteem Builders*. Rolling Hills Estates, CA: Jalmar Press, 1989.

Bradley, B. *Where Do I Belong? A Kid's Guide to Stepfamilies*. Reading, MA: Addison-Wesley, 1982.

Branden, N. *Psychology of Self-Esteem*. Los Angeles: Bantam Books, Nash Publishing Co., 1969.

Branden, N. "What Is Self-Esteem?" First International Conference on Self-Esteem: August 1990, Asker, Norway. Paper presented.

Briggs, D. C. *Your Child's Self-Esteem*. New York: Dolphin Books, Doubleday & Company, 1975.

Briggs, D. C. *Celebrate Yourself*. Garden City, NY: Doubleday, 1977

Brookover, W. B. *Self-Concept of Ability and School Achievement*. East Lansing, MI: Office of Research and Public Info., Michigan State University, 1965.

Buntman, P. H. *How to Live With Your Teenager*. New York: Ballantine Books, 1979.

Buscaglia, L. *Living, Loving & Learning*. Thorofare, NJ: Charles B. Slack, 1982.

Buscaglia, L. *Love*. Thorofare, NJ: Charles B. Slack, 1972.

Canfield, J., and H. C. Wells. *100 Ways to Enhance Self-Concept in the Classroom*. Englewood Cliffs, NJ: Prentice-Hall, 1976.

Cathcart, R. S. *Small Group Communication*. Dubuque, IA: Wm. C. Brown Company, 1979.

Cetron, M. *Schools of the Future*. New York: McGraw-Hill, 1985.

"Children Having Children: Teen Pregnancy in America." *TIME*. December 9, 1985. pp. 78-90.

Chuska, K. R. *Teaching the Process of Thinking, K-12*. Bloomington, Indiana: Phi Delta Kappa Educational Foundation, 1986.

Clems, H., and R. Bean. *Self-Esteem: The Key to Your Child's Well-Being*. New York: Putnam, 1981.

Coopersmith, S. *The Antecedents of Self-Esteem*. San Francisco, CA: W. H. Freeman, 1967.

Covington, M. "Self-Esteem and Failure in School." *The Social Importance of Self-Esteem*. University of California Press, Berkeley, CA, 1989.

Cretcher, D. *Steering Clear*. Minneapolis, MN: Winston, 1982.

Crockenberg, S., and B. Soby. "Self-Esteem and Teenage Pregnancy," *The Social Importance of Self-Esteem*. University of California Press, Berkeley, CA, 1989.

Crow, L. and A. Crow. *How to Study*. New York: Collier Books, 1980.

Curran, D. *Traits of a Healthy Family*. Minneapolis, MN: Winston, 1983.

Danziger, P. *The Cat Ate My Gymsuit*. New York: Dell, 1973.

Davis, L., and J. Davis. *How to Live Almost Happily with Your Teenagers*. Minneapolis, MN: Winston, 1982.

Dillon, J. T. *Teaching and The Art of Questioning*. Bloomington, IN: Phi Delta Kappa Educational Foundation, 1983.

Dishon, D., and P. W. O'Leary. *A Guidebook for Cooperative Learning: A Technique for Creating More Effective Schools*. Holmes Beach, FL: Learning Publications, Inc., 1984.

"Do You Know What Your Children Are Listening To?" *U.S. News & World Report*. October 28, 1985.

Dobson, J. *Preparing for Adolescence*. Santa Ana, CA: Vision House, 1978.

Dodson, F. *How to Discipline With Love*. New York: Rawson Associates, 1977.

Dreikurs, R. *Children: The Challenge*. New York: Hawthorn, 1964.

Drew, N. *Learning the Skills of Peacemaking*. Rolling Hills, CA: Jalmar Press, 1987.

Dyer, W. *What Do You Really Want for Your Children?* New York: William Morrow and Company, Inc., 1985.

Earle, J. *Female Dropouts: A New Perspective*. Alexandria, VA: National Association of State Boards of Education, 1987.

Elkind, D. *All Grown Up and No Place to Go*. Reading, MA: Addison-Wesley, 1984.

"Family Fitness: A Complete Exercise Program for Ages Six to Sixty-Plus." *Reader's Digest*. (Special Report) 1987, p. 2-12.

Fensterheim, H. *Don't Say Yes When You Want to Say No*. New York: Dell Publishing Co., 1975.

Fox, L., and F. Lavin-Weaver. *Unlocking Doors to Self-Esteem*. Rolling Hills Estates, CA: Jalmar Press, 1983.

Freed, A. *TA for Tots,* Revised. Rolling Hills Estates, CA: Jalmar Press, 1991.

Freed, A. *TA for Teens*. Rolling Hills Estates, CA: Jalmar Press, 1976.

Freed, A., and M. Freed. *TA for Kids*. Rolling Hills Estates, CA: Jalmar Press, 1977.

Fromm, Eric. *The Art of Loving*. New York: Bantam, 1963.

Fugitt, E. D. *He Hit Me Back First!* Rolling Hills Estates, CA: Jalmar Press, 1983.

Gall, M. Synthesis of Research on Teachers' Questioning, *Educational Leadership*. November 1984, 40-47.

Gardner, J. E. *The Turbulent Teens*. Los Angeles: Sorrento Press, Inc., 1983.

Gardner, R. *The Boys and Girls Book About Stepfamilies*. New York: Bantam Books, 1982.

Gelb, M. *Present Yourself*. Rolling Hills Estates, CA: Jalmar Press, 1988.

Getzoff, A., and C. McClenahan. *Stepkids: A Survival Guide for Teenagers in Stepfamilies*. New York: Walker and Company, 1984.

Gibbs, J. *Tribes: A Process for Social Development and Cooperative Learning*. Center Source Publications: Santa Rosa, CA, 1987.

Ginott, H. *Teacher and Child*. New York: Avon, 1972.

Gimbel, C. *Why Does Santa Claus Celebrate Christmas?* Rolling Hills Estates, CA: Jalmar Press, 1990.

Glasser, W. *Schools Without Failure*. New York: Harper & Row, 1969.

Gordon, T. *Parent Effectiveness Training*. New York: Peter H. Wyden, 1974.

Gossop, M. "Drug Dependence and Self-Esteem," *International Journal of Addictions,* Vol. II, 1976.

Greenberg, P. *I Know I'm Myself Because . . .* New York: Human Science Press, 1988.

Gribben, T. *Pajamas Don't Matter.* Rolling Hills Estates, CA: Jalmar Press, 1979.

Harris, T. A. *I'm OK—You're OK.* New York: Avon, 1967.

"Has Rock Gone Too Far?" *People Magazine.* September 16, 1985, pp. 47-53.

Haynes-Klassen. *Learning to Live, Learning to Love.* Rolling Hills Estates, CA: Jalmar Press, 1985.

Hill, W. F. *Learning Through Discussion.* Beverly Hills, CA: Sage Publications, 1977.

Holt, J. *How Children Learn.* New York: Delta Books, 1967.

Hyde, M. O. *Parents Divided, Parents Multiplied.* Louisville, KY: Westminster/John Knox Press, 1989.

James, M., and D. Jongeward. *Born to Win.* Menlo Park, CA: Addison-Wesley, 1971.

Jampolsky, G. G. *Teach Only Love.* New York: Bantam, 1983.

Johnson, D. W., and R. T. Johnson *Learning Together and Alone: Cooperative, Competitive and Individualistic Learning,* 4th ed. Englewood Cliffs, NJ: Prentice-Hall, Inc., 1987.

Johnson, D. W., R. T. Johnson, E. J. Holubec, and P. Roy. *Circles of Learning.* ASCD Publications, 1984.

Kagan, S. *Cooperative Learning Resources for Teachers.* Riverside, CA: School of Education, University of California, 1985.

Kalb, J., and Viscott, D. *What Every Kid Should Know.* Boston: Houghton Mifflin, 1974.

Kaplan, H. B. *Self-Attitudes and Deviant Behavior.* Goodyear, Pacific Palisades, CA, 1975.

Kaufman, R. *Identifying and Solving Problems: A System Approach.* San Diego, CA: University Associates, Inc., 1989.

Kehegan, V. A. *SAGE: Self-Awareness Growth Experiences.* Rolling Hills Estates, CA: Jalmar Press, 1989.

Keirsey, D., and M. Bates. *Please Understand Me.* Del Mar, CA: Prometheus Nemesis, 1978.

Kelley, T. M. "Changes in Self-Esteem Among Pre-Delinquent Youths in Voluntary Counseling Relationships." *Juvenile and Family Court Journal.* Vol. 29, May 1978.

"Kids and Cocaine: An Epidemic Strikes Middle America." *Newsweek.* March 17, 1986, pp. 58-63.

Knight, M. E., T. L. Graham, R. A. Juliano, S. R. Miksza, and P. G. Tonnies. *Teaching Children to Love Themselves.* Englewood Cliffs, NJ: Prentice-Hall, 1982.

Kohen-Raz, R. *The Child from 9-13.* Chicago, Illinois: Aldine Adterton, Inc., 1971.

Kreidler, W. *Creative Conflict Resolution: More Than 200 Activities for Keeping Peace in the Classroom.* Glenview, IL: Scott, Foresman and Co., 1984.

Lalli, J. *Feelings Alphabet*. Rolling Hills Estates, CA: Jalmar Press, 1988.

Lansky, D., and S. Dorfman. *How To Survive High School with Minimal Brain Damage*. Minneapolis, MN: Meadowbrook, 1989.

LeShan, E. *What's Going to Happen To Me? When Parents Separate or Divorce*. Four Winds Press, 1978.

Lewis, D., and J. Greene. *Thinking Better*. New York: Rawson, Wade Publishers, Inc., 1982.

Lorayne, H., and J. Lucas. *The Memory Book*. New York: Stein and Day, 1974.

Kuczen, B. *Childhood Stress*. New York: Delacorte, 1982.

Male, M., D. Johnson, R. Johnson, and M. Anderson. *Cooperative Learning and Computers: An Activity Guide for Teachers*. CA: Educational-Apple-Cations, 1987.

Martinelli, K. J. "Thinking Straight About Thinking," *The School Administrator*. No. 44, Jan. 1987, pp. 21-23.

Maslow, A. *Toward a Psychology of Being*. New York: D. Van Nostrand, 1962.

McCabe, M. E., and J. Rhoades. *How to Say What You Mean*. CA: ITA Publications, 1985.

McCullough, C., and R. Mann. *Managing Your Anxiety*. Los Angeles: Tarcher/St. Martin's Press, 1985.

McDaniel, S., and P. Bielen. *Project Self-Esteem*. Rolling Hills Estates, CA: Jalmar Press, 1990.

McKay, M., and P. Fanning. *Self-Esteem*. Oakland, CA: New Harbinger Publications, 1987.

Miller, G. P. *Teaching Your Child To Make Decisions*. New York: Harper & Row, 1984.

Montessori, M. *The Discovery of the Child*. Notre Dame, IN: Fides, 1967.

Naisbitt, J. *Megatrends*. New York: Warner Books, 1982.

Newman, M., and B. Berkowitz. *How To Be Your Own Best Friend*. New York: Random House, 1973.

Neufeld, J. *Lisa, Bright and Dark*. New York: S. G. Phillips, 1969.

Olson, C. B. "Fostering Critical Thinking Skills Through Writing," *Educational Leadership*, November 1984, pp. 28-39.

Palmer, P. *Liking Myself*. San Luis Obispo, CA: Impact, 1977.

Palmer, Pat, *The Mouse, The Monster, and Me*. San Luis Obispo, CA: Impact, 1977.

Peal, N. V. *You Can If You Think You Can*. Pawling, NY: Foundation for Christian Living, 1974.

Pelletier, K. *Mind as Healer, Mind as Slayer*. New York: Delacorte, 1977.

Postman, N. *The Disappearance of Childhood*. New York: Delacorte Press, 1982.

Raths, L. E., et al. *Teaching for Thinking: Theories, Strategies, and Activities for the Classroom*. New York: Teachers College Press, 1986.

Richards, A. K., and I. Willis. *Boy Friends, Girl Friends, Just Friends.* Atheneum, NY: McClelland & Stewart, Ltd., 1979.

Samples, B. *Metaphoric Mind.* Rolling Hills Estates, CA: Jalmar Press, 1991.

Samples, B. *Openmind/Wholemind.* Rolling Hills Estates, CA: Jalmar Press, 1987.

Samson, R. W. *Thinking Skills: A Guide to Logic and Comprehension.* Stamford, CT: Innovative Sciences, Inc., 1981.

Satir, V. *Peoplemaking.* Palo Alto, CA: Science & Behavior Books Inc., 1972.

Schmuck, R., and P. Schmuck. *A Humanistic Psychology of Education: Making the School Everybody's House.* Palo Alto, CA: Mayfield Publishing Co., 1974.

Schneiderwind, N., and E. Davidson. *Open Minds to Equity: A Sourcebook of Learning Activities to Promote Race, Sex, Class and Age Equity.* NJ: Prentice-Hall, 1983.

Schuller, R. *Self-Esteem: The New Reformation.* Waco, TX: Word Books, Inc., 1982

Schriner, C. *Feel Better Now.* Rolling Hills Estates, CA: Jalmar Press, 1990.

Sexton, T. G., and D. R. Poling. "Can Intelligence Be Taught?" Bloomingdale, IN: Phi Delta Kappa Educational Foundation, 1973.

Sheehy, G. *Pathfinders,* New York: Morrow, 1981.

Sheinkin, D. *Food, Mind and Mood.* New York: Warner Books, 1980.

Shles, L. *Aliens in My Nest.* Rolling Hills Estates, CA: Jalmar Press, 1988.

Shles, L. *Moths & Mothers/Feathers & Fathers.* Rolling Hills Estates, CA: Jalmar Press, 1989.

Shles, L. *Do I Have to Go to School Today?* Rolling Hills Estates, CA: Jalmar Press, 1989.

Shles, L. *Hugs & Shrugs.* Rolling Hills Estates, CA: Jalmar Press, 1987.

Shles, L. *Hoots & Toots & Hairy Brutes?* Rolling Hills Estates, CA: Jalmar Press, 1989.

Silberstein, W. *Helping Your Child Grow Slim.* New York: Simon & Schuster. 1982.

Simpson, B. K. *Becoming Aware of Values.* La Mesa, CA: Pennant Press, 1973.

Skoguland, E. R. *To Anger With Love.* New York: Harper & Row, 1977.

Smith, M. J. *When I Say No I Feel Guilty.* New York: Bantam, 1975.

Stainback, W., and S. Stainback. *How to Help Your Child Succeed in School.* Minneapolis, MN: Meadowbrook, 1988.

Steffenhagen, R. A., and J. D. Burns. *The Social Dynamics of Self-Esteem.* New York, NY: Praeger, 1987.

Steiner, C. *The Original Warm Fuzzy Tale.* Rolling Hills Estates, CA: Jalmar Press, 1977.

"Teenage Fathers." *Psychology Today.* December 1985, pp. 66-70.

Ungerleider, D. *Reading, Writing and Rage.* Rolling Hills Estates, CA: Jalmar Press, 1985.

Vennard, J. *Synergy.* Novato, CA: Academic Therapy Publications, 1978.

Viscott, D. *The Language of Feelings.* New York: Pocket Books, 1976.

Vitale, B. M. *Unicorns Are Real.* Rolling Hills Estates, CA: Jalmar Press, 1982.

Vitale, B. M. *Free Flight.* Rolling Hills Estates, CA: Jalmar Press, 1986.

Wahlross, S. *Family Communication.* New York: Macmillan Publishing Co., Inc., 1974.

Warren, N. C. *Make Anger Your Ally.* Garden City, NY: Doubleday 1983.

Wassmer, A. C. *Making Contact.* New York: Dial Press, 1978.

Whitely, J. *Moral Character Development of College Students.* University of Irvine, Irvine, CA, 1980.

Wilson, J. "Motivation, Modeling, and Altruism," *Journal of Personality and Social Psychology*, Vol. 34, Dec. 1976.

Winn, M. *Children Without Childhood.* New York: Pantheon Books, 1981.

Winter, A., and R. Winter. *Build Your Brain Power.* NY: St. Martin's, 1986.

Wright, E. *Good Morning Class — I Love You!* Rolling Hills Estates, CA: Jalmar Press, 1989.

Wyckoff, J, and B. Unell. *Discipline Without Shouting or Spanking.* Minneapolis, MN: Meadowbrook, 1988.

Young, E. *I Am a Blade of Grass.* Rolling Hills Estates, CA: Jalmar Press, 1989.

Youngs, Bettie B. *Stress in Children: How to Recognize, Avoid and Overcome It.* New York: Avon, 1985.

Youngs, Bettie B. *Helping Your Teenager Deal With Stress: A Guide to the Adolescent Years.* Los Angeles: Tarcher/St. Martin's, 1986.

Youngs, Bettie B. *A Stress Management Guide for Young People.* San Diego, CA: Learning Tools, 1988.

Youngs, Bettie B. *Friendship Is Forever, Isn't It?* San Diego, CA: Learning Tools, 1990.

Youngs, Bettie B. *Goal Setting Skills for Young People.* San Diego, CA: Learning Tools, 1989.

Youngs, Bettie B. *Problem Solving Skills for Children.* San Diego, CA: Learning Tools, 1989.

Youngs, Bettie B. *You and Self-Esteem: It's The Key to Happiness & Success.* Rolling Hills Estates, CA: Jalmar Press: 1992.

Youngs, Bettie B. *Stress Management for Educators.* Rolling Hills Estates, CA: Jalmar Press: 1992.

Youngs, Bettie B. *Enhancing The Educator's Self-Esteem: Criteria #1.* Rolling Hills Estates, CA: Jalmar Press: 1992.

HELP ORGANIZATIONS

Many organizations, some with toll-free 800 phone numbers, provide helpful information, among them:

Alcoholics Anonymous
World Services, Inc.
468 Park Ave. South
New York, NY 10016
(212) 686-1100

Al-Ateen, Al-Anon Family Group Headquarters
P.O. Box 182
New York, NY 10159-0182

Alcoholics Anonymous is an international fellowship of men and women who share the common problem of alcoholism. Family members of alcoholics can receive help through groups associated with Alcoholics Anonymous, mainly Al-Anon and Al-Ateen. Al-Ateen chapters are listed in some phone books or you can contact a local Al-Anon group for more information.

Big Brothers/Big Sisters of America
230 North Thirteenth St.
Philadelphia, PA 19107
(215) 567-7000

Big Brother/Sisters of America is a national youth-serving organization based on the concept of a one-to-one relationship between an adult volunteer and an at-risk child, usually from a one-parent family. With more than 495 agencies located nationwide, the organization is dedicated to providing children and youth with adult role models and mentors who help enrich the children's lives, as well as their own, through weekly interaction. Volunteers go through a screening process before being accepted into the program, and professional caseworkers provide assistance, support, and on-going supervision for all matches. Check the white pages of your phone book for the agency nearest you.

Boys' National Hotline
(800) 448-3000 (toll-free)
This hotline provides emergency crisis counseling.

Family Service America (FSA)
11700 West Lake Park Drive
Park Place
Milwaukee, WI 53224
(414) 359-1040

FSA is a membership organization of agencies that deals with family problems serving more than 1000 communities throughout the United States and Canada. Member agencies serve families and individuals through counseling, advocacy, and family life education. Consult the phone book for the agency nearest you.

National Center for Missing and Exploited Children
2101 Wilson Blvd., Ste. 550
Arlington, VA 22021
(703) 235-3900

The center assists families, citizens' groups, law enforcement agencies, and governmental institutions. The center also has a toll-free number for reporting information that could lead to the location and recovery of a missing child. The number is (800) 843-5678.

National Child Abuse Hotline
P.O. Box 630
Hollywood, CA 90028
(800) 422-4453 (toll-free)

The National Child Abuse Hotline handles crises calls and information and offers referrals to every county in the United States. The hotline is manned by professionals holding a master's degree or Ph.D. in psychology. The hotline also provides literature about child abuse prevention. This program is sponsored by Childhelp USA, which is located in Woodland, CA.

National Clearinghouse for Alcohol and Drug Information (NCADI)
P.O. Box 2345
Rockville, MD 20852
(301) 468-2600
(800) 729-6686 (toll-free)

NCADI is the information component of the Office for Substance Abuse Prevention (OSAP) of the U.S. Dept. of Health and Human Services. The clearinghouse maintains an inventory of hundreds of publications developed by Federal agencies and private sector organizations. Most publications are free or are available in bulk quantities for a small fee. NCADI also offers fact verification, video loans, and dissemination of grant announcements and application kits. NCADI provides access to the Prevention Materials Database, an online computer database designed to help select specific items from the NCADI's collection of prevention materials. NCADI publishes "Prevention Pipeline," a bimonthly publication that contains the latest information about research, resources, and activities within the prevention field.

National Council for Self-Esteem
P.O. Box 277877
Sacramento, CA 95827-7877
(916) 455-NCSE
(916) 455-2000

The NCSE is dedicated to promoting and developing quality self-esteem information. The NCSE's mission is to spread the ethics of self-esteem throughout the United States. The organization seeks to ensure that self-esteem information is readily available to those who seek it. Operating as Self-Esteem Central, the NSCE collects information on the best self-esteem curriculums, school programs, drug prevention programs, drop-out prevention programs, study courses, videos, and audio-tape programs. Self-Esteem Central houses the National Self-Esteem Library, reported to be be the largest collection of self-esteem resources in the world. The library offers research assistance and audio-tape programs. The "Self-Esteem Today" newsletter offers the latest in new ideas to develop self-esteem, including current research, model programs, and upcoming conference information. More than 50 local Self-Esteem Councils exist in 20 states. For more information, or to start a council in your city, write the NSCE.

National Institute on Drug Abuse
P.O. Box 100
Summit, NJ 07901
(800) COCAINE (toll-free)

The National Institute on Drug Abuse hotline is a confidential drug abuse treatment referral service. The hotline provides information on local referrals and help for drug abusers and other concerned individuals.

National Runaway Switch Board
(800) 621-4000 (toll-free)

National Youth Work Alliance
1346 Connecticut Ave, N.W.
Washington, D.C. 20036
Offers local referrals for runaway or teen crisis shelters.

Parents Anonymous (P.A.)
7120 Franklin
Los Angeles, CA 90046
(800) 421-0353 (toll-free, outside CA)
(800) 352-0386 (toll-free, CA)

P.A. is a self-help program for parents under stress and for abused children. There are no fees and no one is required to reveal his or her name. Group members support and encourage each other in searching out positive alternatives to the abusive behavior in their lives. To locate a P.A. in you area, call the toll-free hotline numbers listed above.

Crisis counseling and information available 24 hours a day, seven days a week.

Suicide Prevention

Almost every state and major city has one or more suicide hotlines and/or suicide prevention centers. For centers in your area, check with your phone operator, or the State, City, or County Health & Human Services headings in your phone book.

United Way, Inc.

Check the phone book to contact the United Way organization in your area to find the Family Services Agency nearest you. These organizations offer a variety of family counseling services.

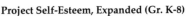

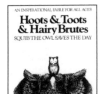

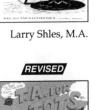
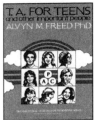
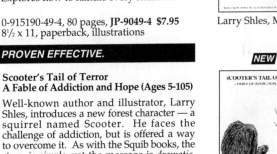

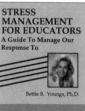
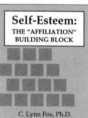